done in a day
STORAGE solutions

done in a day
STORAGE
solutions

STEWART WALTON

MARSHALL PUBLISHING • LONDON

A Marshall Edition
Conceived, edited and designed by
Marshall Editions Ltd
The Orangery
161 New Bond Street
London W1Y 9PA

First published in the UK in 1998 by Marshall Publishing Ltd

Hardback ISBN 1-84028-191-X
Paperback ISBN 1-84028-123-5

9 8 7 6 5 4 3 2 1

Project Editor: Esther Labi
Photographer: John Freeman
Consultant: Sally Walton
Illustrator: Kuo Kang Chen
Designer: Vicky Holmes/ Joanna Stawarz
DtP Editor: Lesley Gilbert
Managing Editor: Claire Currie
Editorial Coordinator: Rebecca Clunes
Art Director: Sean Keogh
Production: James Bann

Text written by Esther Labi

Originated in Singapore by Master Image
Printed and bound in Italy

CONTENTS

INTRODUCTION

Forever tripping over toys, or bumping into clutter? Are you always looking for house keys? Can you never find a piece of adhesive tape, or an envelope when you want one? Within these pages you will find lots of ideas to help you organise the space in your home and turn chaos into order.

The first step to a more organised lifestyle is to take a look around you and establish what areas are most cluttered and need most attention. It may be helpful to make lists of what is lying around and getting in the way. Perhaps you have nowhere to store important documents, hats, coats and shoes, kitchenware or cosmetics. Maybe it's mostly books and magazines that cause your clutter and are crying out for some organisation. Once you have listed the type of objects that need storing, analyse your list. What are the reasons for storing them? What do you want from your storage? How frequently do you need to access the items you have stored?

When you have identified and analysed your needs, it's time to consider the solutions available. Take a quick look through the 12 projects of this book and see if you can find something that is either exactly what you are looking for, or something that will give you an idea for a starting point, an idea that you can then adapt to suit your specific needs.

If kitchen storage is required, the **glass rack** is practical and space saving, while the **kitchen shelves** provide both hanging and shelf space, and there are two styles to choose from. If you'd like to conceal your shelves rather than display them, look at the **picture box cupboard**, which allows you to use your valuable wall space both decoratively and functionally and gives your framed prints a double use.

If you think you don't have room in your home to create storage, look in particular for "dead space". This includes the space under beds, under staircases, above bathroom fixtures and underneath existing shelves. We made the **hide-away carts** and the **understair tidy** with this in mind. And don't think that storage solutions are just for the home. The **bathroom organiser** and the hanging **shoe tidy** can be used for travelling too. The shoe tidy will fit on any hotel coat hanger and the bathroom organiser can be rolled up to fit into a suitcase or into an overnight bag for an impromptu weekend trip.

Children have their own needs when it comes to storage, and it is important that they learn the responsibilities of tidying up after themselves at an early age. To encourage this, storage must be accessible (at a low height) as well as providing an appealing focus in a child's room. You'll find the **child's box seat** and the **child's valet** both fun and practical, especially when they are painted in bright colours or blackboard paint.

This book can be either loosely followed, or followed to the letter, letting the steps guide you. Where possible, suggestions are made as to how to make the projects more flexible to your own requirements. Two projects that can be customised to your own needs are the **multipurpose hallstand** (make as many shelves and hanging pegs as you like) and the **desktop organiser**, which has some adjustable shelving, so you can adapt it to meet your changing circumstances.

Whichever storage solution you choose to make, don't forget to put your personal stamp on it, because the best storage suits your needs as well as your personality, lifestyle and taste.

A NOTE ABOUT MEASUREMENTS:

All the measurements that appear in this book are in imperial measures, that is, in inches and feet. The reason being that many building and tool supplies, such as drill bits, screws tools and wood lengths are still identified by the old imperial name or numbered under an old system. However, if you prefer to use metric, there is a conversion table for inches and millimetres at the back of the book, on page 110.

A NOTE ABOUT DRILL BITS AND SCREWS:

Drill bits were once labelled under the Standard System, which used numbers and letters to denote size. Some manufacturers give both metric and Standard equivalents on their packaging. If not, there is also a table of Standard drill bit sizes and their metric and imperial equivalents on page 110; so you are sure to find the correct size. When purchasing screws, note that all screws in the book refer to wood screws, not machine screws.

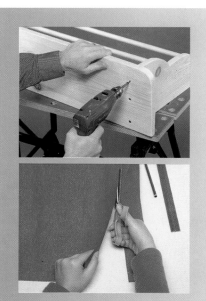

Now that you are ready to attempt your first project, keep the following safety procedures in mind at all times:

❖ If any step suggest protective clothing, such as goggles or gloves, for certain activities *do* wear them; remember, accidents do happen

❖ Always keep powertools unplugged whilst they are not in use;

❖ When working with a craft knife keep your steadying hand well away from and behind your cutting hand;

❖ If you are working outdoors make sure that any powertool cables are kept clear of water;

❖ When using a sewing machine, keep your guiding fingers well away from the needle.

❖ Only cut MDF (Medium Density Fibreboard) in a well-ventilated area and wear the correct type of breathing mask.

HOW THIS BOOK WORKS

A brief introduction and description of each project

List of the equipment needed for each project

Exploded diagram shows how elements fit together

Step-by-step photographs provide a visual reference to accompany the text

'Professional Tip' boxes offer expert guidance on achieving the best results

Descriptive text accompanies each photograph, to ensure you know exactly what you are doing

Information boxes provide useful tips on products and procedures

Close-up photographs of the finished projects show the end result

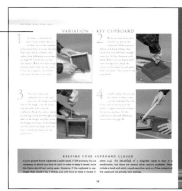

A variation of each project provides an interesting alternative

Variations are also illustrated in detail

KITCHEN SHELVES

Clear clutter from your kitchen worktop and instead, display it on an attractive and practical set of shelves. For country-style kitchens, make the shelves in rustic-looking stained pine, or make a sleeker modern variation in varnished mdf.

EQUIPMENT

Jigsaw

Pencil

Bradawl

Paintbrush

Power drill/
Screwdriver

Sandpaper
(medium and fine)

Hammer

Hacksaw

Cardboard (for template)

Crosscut saw

Tenon saw

Round object to
use as a guide

Clamp

No.5 drill bit

¾-inch drill bit

Combination square

MATERIALS

❖ Piece of pine, 8½ by ¾ inches, 9 feet long

❖ Doweling, ¾ inch in diameter, 7½ feet long

❖ No. 6 screws, 1¾-inches long

❖ No. 6 screws, 1½-inches long

❖ Panel pins, 1½-inches long

❖ Quick-drying wood-coloured filler

❖ Blue emulsion paint, or a water-based glaze or colourwash

VARIATION

❖ Sheet of ¾-inch mdf, 2½ by 3 feet

❖ No. 6 screws, 1¾-inches long

❖ Metal hanging rail, ¾ inch in diameter, 7½ feet long

❖ Six metal ends and screws to fit

❖ Varnish or paint

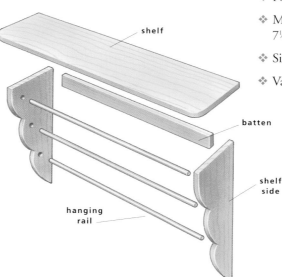

shelf

batten

shelf
side

hanging
rail

STARTING OUT - STEPS 1 TO 4

1 Measure one length of pine 36 inches long and two lengths at 21 inches. Cut them out with a crosscut saw. The longer piece is the top of the shelf and the two shorter lengths will be the sides of the shelf.

2 Enlarge the shape marked template A on page 16 on a photocopying machine by 270 percent. Copy it onto a piece of cardboard and cut this out. Make sure that you also copy the three crosses on the template. Lay the cardboard template on one of the shelf sides and trace around it in pencil. Repeat on the other shelf side.

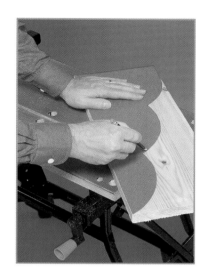

3 Place a shelf side on a workbench or work surface and clamp it so that it will not move (see below). If you are unable to clamp the wood, you may need someone to help you hold the wood steady. Using a jigsaw, cut out both shelf sides.

4 Lay the longer piece of wood on the workbench or work surface. Decide which edge will be the front of your shelf. Using a mug or any round object as a guide, pencil curves around the front two corners of the shelf. Then cut around these curves with a jigsaw.

PROFESSIONAL TIP

When clamping wood to a workbench or work surface, place a scrap of wood between the clamp and the wood you are cutting. This will avoid marking or damaging your wood with the jaws of the clamp. The most common clamp used for this purpose is a G-clamp, which is a metal clamp with an adjustable grip and is shaped like the letter G. These clamps are sold in a large range of sizes so if you are buying one, make sure the size you buy will be useful for a number of different tasks.

PUTTING IT TOGETHER – STEPS 5 TO 8

5 Using a piece of medium-grade sandpaper, sand the curves of the shelf. For a very smooth finish, follow with a fine-grade sandpaper. Sand the two shelf sides in the same way.

6 Place the template on one of the shelf sides. To mark where the dowels will go press through the cardboard with a bradawl at each marked cross. Then turn the template over and place it on the other shelf side. Mark it in the same way. Make sure that when you stand the shelf sides up, the bradawl marks are facing each other.

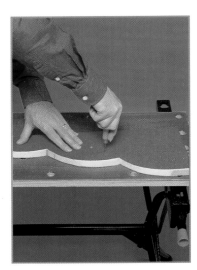

7 To make rebates for the dowels, place a shelf side on the workbench or work surface and clamp it in place. Using a power drill and a ¾ inch wood or auger bit, drill a hole ⅜-inch deep on each of the bradawl marks. Use a depth gauge or some masking tape to mark the depth of the hole (see page 89). Do the same for the other shelf side. Then mark the centre of each drilled hole with a nail following the instructions below.

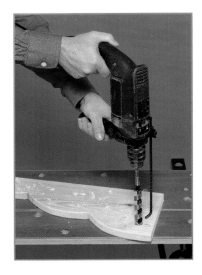

8 On the long piece of wood measure and mark a point 2 ¾ inches in from each side at the back of the shelf. Place one of the shelf sides on one of the points, making sure that the dowel rebates are facing toward the centre of the shelf. Check the shelf side is square using a combination square. Then trace around the base of the shelf side with a pencil. Repeat at the other marked point.

MAKING THE SHELVES SECURE

The holes drilled in step 7 are for the dowels. In step 15 you have to secure the dowels by screwing through the sides of the shelf into the centre of each dowel. To mark the centre of the dowel rebates, lightly hammer a nail through each dowel rebate you drilled, so that it goes through to the other side. Turn the shelf sides over and at the point where the nail came through, use a drill to countersink each one. When you place the screws into the doweling, the ends of the screws will be flush.

PUTTING IT TOGETHER – STEPS 9 TO 12

9 The long shelf is attached to the shelf sides with glue and screws, so you need to drill pilot holes for each screw. Within each of the outlines, mark points 1, 4 and 6 ½ inches from the back of the shelf. Drill holes at each of these points using a No.5 drill bit. Then turn the shelf over and countersink each pilot hole.

10 To calculate the length of the dowels, measure between the two outlines marked on the shelf. The doweling should be this length plus ¾ inch; in this case, 29¾ inches. Measure and cut three lengths of dowels with a tenon saw.

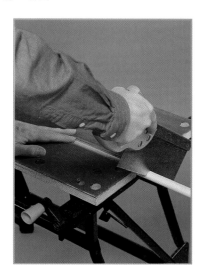

11 A length of batten is required to support the shelf. It fits in between the two sides. The batten should be about 2½ inches wide and the length should be the same as the distance between the two pencil outlines, in this case, 29 inches. You should have enough wood left over to make one to fit.

12 To secure the finished shelves to the wall, you will have to screw through the batten. The position of the pilot holes will depend on the type of wall you have, in this case, pilot holes were drilled 2 inches in from each end. Countersink these holes so that the screws will be flush with the wood.

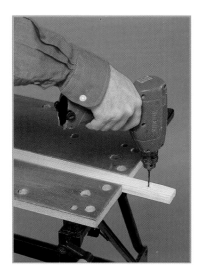

CUTTING ON THE WASTEWOOD

To keep cut lengths accurate, always measure carefully with a straight ruler and a very sharp pencil – a blunt pencil can result in measurements that are slightly askew. After marking a length of wood, you should cut on the wastewood side of the line you have drawn. This means you should cut on the side of the line that is not part of the length you are cutting. To get lengths absolutely accurate, cut a length on the wastewood side, and then you can sand some of the wood away to the exact requirement.

FINISHING IT OFF – STEPS 13 TO 16

13 To assemble the shelves, hold one of the sides against the long shelf on the pencil line. Using a power screwdriver, screw each of the three pilot holes with 1¾-inch screws. Add a dab of wood glue to the ends of the dowels and place them into the rebates. Align the other shelf side against the long shelf, attach the dowels and screw the shelf side into place.

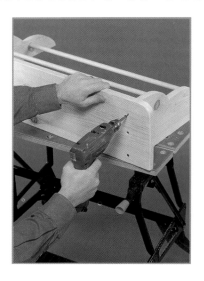

14 Place some wood glue along the length of batten and at each end and place the batten at the back of the shelf. Make sure the countersunk holes are facing you. Then hammer a 1½-inch panel pin into the corner of the side of the shelf, to further secure the batten. Do the same on the other side of the shelf.

15 To make the hanging space on the shelves extra secure, screw 1½-inch screws through the pilot holes into the dowelling. Cover all the screw and nail heads with a quick-drying filler. (This usually dries in about 10 minutes, but always follow the manufacturer's instructions.) Then, rub over all the filled areas with sandpaper.

16 (Before painting you may wish to protect your work surface with an old sheet or newspaper.) Mix some emulsion paint with water to a thin consistency or use a commercially prepared water-based glaze or colourwash paint. Paint the shelves and the dowels with long brush strokes. The brush marks will add to its rustic look. To make your shelves look aged, lightly sand around the edges when the paint has dried.

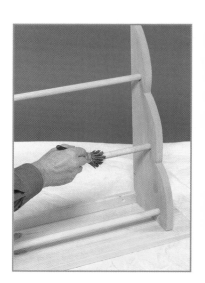

PAINTING PINE

It is important to paint some type of finish on to the surface of the pine, be it varnish, emulsion or a water-based glaze. A painted finish, as opposed to a wax finish, will protect the wood from the different conditions in the kitchen, which can vary from cool to warm to hot and humid when cooking. Before applying a finish, make sure you prepare the surface. This includes looking for any cracks and blemishes that need filling as well as applying knotting to visible knots in the wood to prevent resin from bleeding through the paint.

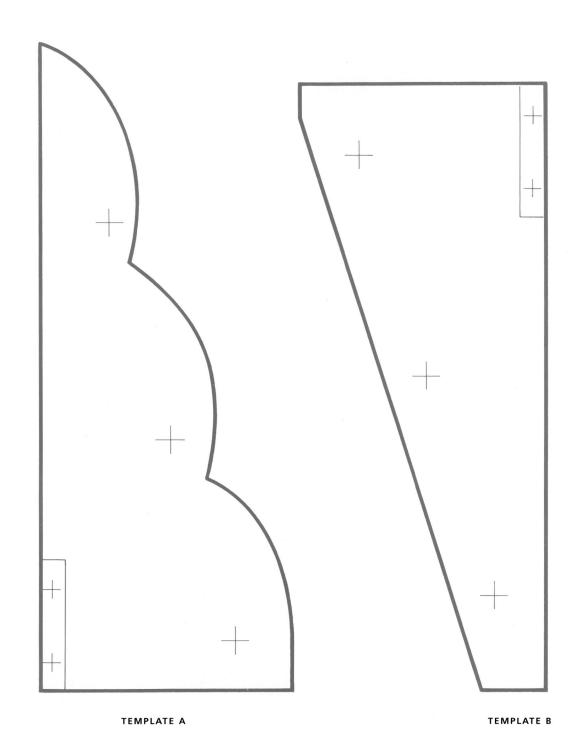

TEMPLATE A   TEMPLATE B

VARIATION - MODERN MDF

1 On the sheet of mdf, measure and cut out one piece measuring 8¾ by 36 inches and two pieces at 7¾ by 20 inches for the sides. For the batten, you will need to cut out a piece 4 by 29 inches. Then, enlarge template B on page 16 by 270 percent and copy this onto a piece of cardboard. Cut out the cardboard and trace around this twice on the mdf. Cut out two sides with a jigsaw.

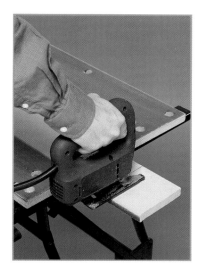

2 Place the cardboard template over each of the cut-out sides in turn and locate the positions of the pilot holes for the hanging rails as well as those in the corner of the template, which are for the batten. Mark the wood at each of these points by pressing a bradawl through the template.

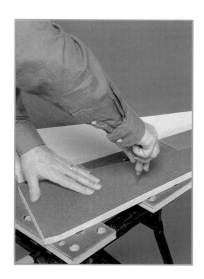

3 Working on one side piece at a time, centre the metal rail ends over the three bradawl marks. Break the surface of the mdf through each of the holes for screws, then screw the metal rail ends in position. The size of the screws will depend on the size of the rail ends you have. Then do the same for the other side piece.

4 Place one of the side pieces on the top shelf, 3 inches in from one side and against one long side. Trace around its width in pencil. Within this guideline, drill three evenly spaced pilot holes, making sure that the first pilot hole is at least 1½ inches from the edge of the wood. Repeat this on the other side, then countersink all the pilot holes.

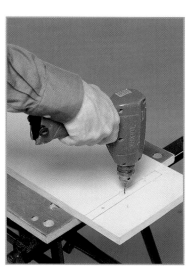

USING POWER TOOLS

Before using any power tools, always familiarize yourself with how they work. Make sure that the flex is kept safely away from the working parts and for additional safety use a circuit-breaker, in case you accidentally cut through the flex. Practise new or difficult cuts on a scrap of wood and only work on the real pieces when you are confident of your ability. If you are not sure about using a particular tool, seek professional advice from an expert or ask someone who does know how to use it to help you.

FINISHING IT OFF - 5 TO 8

5 Measure the hanging rail and mark three lengths of 29 inches. Clamp the hanging rail to your workbench, or get someone to help you hold it secure and cut the rail with a junior hacksaw.

6 To assemble the shelves, hold the shelf side against the top shelf and secure it with 1¾-inch screws in each of the three pilot holes. Place the metal rails in their ends and then attach the other side to the top shelf in the same way (see below). Make sure you place the top shelf on the sides so that the countersunk holes are uppermost.

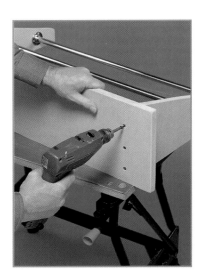

7 Fix a batten to the back of the shelf by placing two screws in the pilot holes you made earlier on each side. For a neat finish, make sure you countersink the pilot holes first. Then rub over all the cut edges and sharp corners with coarse sandpaper. For a professional look, finish with fine sandpaper.

8 Finally, it is important to seal the mdf. You can do this with a couple of coats of matt or gloss varnish, or alternatively, with a painted finish. This could range from a simple flat colour to a more adventurous finish, such as metallic paint.

PROFESSIONAL TIP

By assembling one side of the shelves to the main shelf, then adding the hanging rails and then the other side, you will be able to secure the hanging rails. However, if your hanging rails are cut slightly long, the pilot holes in the main shelf will not align with the side piece below it. If this happens, you can file down the lengths of hanging rails with a half-round file. If the hanging rails are too short, you will have to either recut new hanging rails, or fill the pilot holes and drill new ones.

MULTIPURPOSE HALLSTAND

Hats, coats, bags and umbrellas can all be neatly stored in this up-to-the-minute version of the old-fashioned hallstand. With lots of hanging room and its neat slatted shelving, it is entirely practical as well as being a decorative feature.

EQUIPMENT

¾-inch drill bit

No.7 drill bit

No.5 drill bit

Countersink bit

Sandpaper
(medium and fine)

Combination square

Power drill/
Screwdriver

Crosscut saw

Pencil

Paintbrush

Tenon saw

Pin hammer

MATERIALS

❖ Six 6-foot lengths of prepared pine, 1½ by 1½ inches

❖ Six 6-foot lengths of pine, 1¼ by ⅝ inch

❖ Piece of 4 by 1 inch pine, 3 feet long

❖ Piece of 6 by 1 inch pine, 4 feet long

❖ Doweling, ¾ inch in diameter, 3 feet long

❖ Wood glue

❖ No. 6 screws, 1½ inches long

❖ No. 8 screws, 2 inches long

❖ Panel pins, 1 inch long

❖ Wood-coloured filler

❖ 2 wooden drawer pulls

❖ Clear satin varnish or woodstain

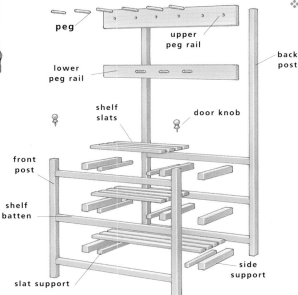

peg

upper
peg rail

lower
peg rail

back
post

shelf
slats

door knob

front
post

shelf
batten

side
support

slat support

STARTING OUT ~ STEPS 1 TO 4

1 To make the two front posts of the hallstand, measure two lengths of 32 inches on one of the 6-foot lengths of 1½ by 1½. You can use a combination square to help you keep your lines straight if you wish. Cut out these pieces with a tenon saw. The back posts will be made of two of the 6-foot lengths, so you do not have to measure or cut these.

2 To make the upper peg rail, measure 40 inches on the 6-by-1-inch pine and cut this out with a crosscut saw. The lower peg rail is made from the 3-foot length of 4-by-1-inch pine.

3 The shelves will be fixed to the front and back posts, so it is important that they are attached to all the posts at the exact same height – otherwise they will slope. From one end of a post, draw a line at 2⅝, 5⅜ and 28 inches, using a combination square to help you. Then, place a width of wood on each line and trace its width. Place each of the remaining lengths against this post and copy all the lines. It is best to do one post at a time, for accuracy.

4 Each of the posts will have more than one side support attached to it, so you need to see the guidelines you have drawn on more than one side. Using a combination square, extend each guideline carefully until you have drawn around the entire post.

PROFESSIONAL TIP

When working on these projects, it is important that you are comfortable and can move around your work area freely and without having to climb over clutter. Make sure the area is tidy and that you have enough room to lay the wood flat.

When sawing wood, position and hold it firmly, at a comfortable height on a stable object such as a box or stool, workbench or a purpose-made sawhorse. If you are working outside, make sure that you clear away any garden debris which could trip you as you work.

PUTTING IT TOGETHER - STEPS 5 TO 8

5 On a 6-foot length of 1½ by 1½ inch pine measure eight lengths of 9 inches. Cut each piece out with a tenon saw. Six of these lengths are the side support pieces and two lengths will form the divider for the umbrella stand.

6 Each of the posts will take two screws, so you need to carefully measure the position of the pilot holes so that they don't intersect. Lay a post on your work surface. On one set of guidelines, measure ⅜ inch in from the guideline on your right-hand side, making sure it is in the centre of the wood. Drill a hole through the post at this point, and repeat for each of the remaining two sets of guidelines.

7 Then, turn the wood over one turn so that you are on an adjacent side. This time, measure ⅜ inch in from the guideline on your left hand side, in the centre of the wood. Drill a hole at this point through the wood, and repeat on the two other guidelines. Countersink the holes on one side, then turn the wood over one turn and countersink the holes on that side. (Make sure that the countersunk holes are adjacent to each other, not opposite.)

8 On the upper peg rail, measure 3 inches in from each short side. Place a side support next to the line, so that it is closer to the centre of the wood, rather than the edge. Trace the width of the wood. Remove the batten and, keeping within these guidelines, measure 1 inch in from the long edges of the wood. Mark these points in pencil and drill through the wood with a No.5 drill bit. Then countersink the holes (on the front side).

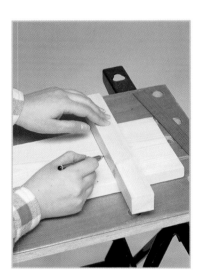

GOOD DRILLING

A power drill is probably one of the most useful tools in your toolbox. Apart from making holes in wood, you can buy special drill bits for metal and masonry work. Always drill through the most important side of the wood, as the side of the wood the drill comes through can get a jagged edge. If you are drilling through a thick surface, remove the drill and blow out the dust, to prevent the drill bit from getting clogged. When you have finished drilling, never touch the drill bit, as they can become hot enough to burn you.

PUTTING IT TOGETHER - STEPS 9 TO 12

9 To assemble the stand, you need to fix the two front posts to the shelf supports. Lay the two posts on a work surface and check that the countersunk holes are facing frontward and outward. Place three shelf supports against one of the front posts at the guidelines drawn in Step 3. Apply some wood glue to the first join and fix the screws in the pilot holes. Attach the other post in the same way.

10 Now make the back section in the same way, checking that the countersunk holes are facing frontward and outward. If your work surface is not large enough, you can work on the floor, but remember to protect it with an old sheet. Use a combination square to check that the front and back sections are square.

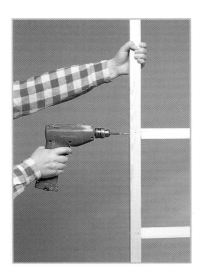

11 Attach the side supports to the front section, gluing each piece of wood first. Hold each one steady and fix 2-inch screws into the wood through the pilot holes.

12 You can now attach the back section to the side supports. You may need somebody to help you hold the front and back sections steady as you join them together with 2-inch screws.

PROFESSIONAL TIP

Each of the four posts of the hallstand take two screws. The way to drill pilot holes for these screws so that they will not intersect is described in Steps 6 and 7. When you assemble your hallstand, and in particular in Steps 9 to 12, make sure that the pilot holes are the same height on the front of the front posts. This is so that from a distance, the screws in the front of the hallstand will not be different heights. Of course, if you intend to cover the screws and paint the hallstand, it does not matter which way they face.

PUTTING IT TOGETHER – STEPS 13 TO 16

13 Then, place a width of batten against the short side of the lower peg rail and trace its width. Keeping within the centre of these guidelines, measure 1 inch in from each long edge and mark these points. Drill pilot holes at each point and countersink them on the front side. Make pilot holes on the other side in the same way.

14 On both peg rails draw a faint pencil line along the length of the wood, just above the middle. Decide how many pegs you need and mark on the line where they will go. We used six pegs on the upper peg rail and three on the lower rail, and spaced them out so that a lower peg was between two of the upper rail pegs. Cut the dowel into 3-inch lengths for each peg required.

15 For each peg, drill a hole at an angle (see below) with a ¾-inch drill bit, using a jig to help you. Make sure you place the jig over each pencil mark so that the pegs will point upward.

16 Sand the edges of the pegs to a smooth finish. Apply a generous amount of wood glue to the end of each peg and slide each peg into a hole, holding the peg in place until the glue dries sufficiently to hold it securely.

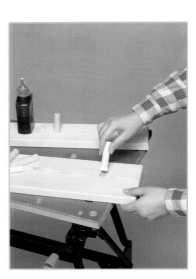

USING A JIG

A jig is used here when drilling holes for the pegs so that the pegs will point slightly upward when they are placed in the holes. This helps stop heavy coats from slipping off the pegs. To make a jig, drill a hole at a slight angle through an offcut of pine. You will need to either clamp it at a slight angle or get someone to help you hold it. Then, clamp the offcut of wood to the peg rail over each pencilled mark and use the hole in the wood to guide the drill. Make sure the jig is around the right way each time.

PUTTING IT TOGETHER – STEPS 17 TO 20

17 Place the upper rail against the two back posts so that the top edge of the rail is aligned with the top of the posts. (You may need to ask someone to help you, or you can lay the hallstand down on a flat surface.) Fix the upper peg rail in position with wood glue and a 1½ inch screw in each pilot hole. Add the lower peg rail in the same way at a suitable height (we measured 17 inches down from the top of the back posts).

18 To make the umbrella section, measure 10½ inches in from the right side of the stand and mark the centre of the uppermost shelf support at the front. Drill a pilot hole at this point with a No.5 drill bit. Do the same on the uppermost shelf support at the back. Place a 9-inch length of wood between these two holes, checking that it is square. Fix into place with wood glue and a 2-inch screw in each hole.

19 To make the shelf slats, first measure the distance between the battens for the three shelves. To be accurate, you should measure each shelf as they will vary slightly. Then, cut four lengths for each shelf from the lengths of 1¼-by-⅝-inch pine.

20 The shelf slats are supported at both ends. Measure and cut out six 9-inch lengths from the 1¼-by-⅝-inch pine. To attach each slat support, you need to drill pilot holes through the side supports. Draw a line along the centre of the side supports. Drill two, evenly spaced pilot holes *below* this line with a No.7 drill bit. (When the slats are placed on top, they should be flush with the side supports.)

PROFESSIONAL TIP

Make sure you use the right size screwdriver for the screw you are using by checking the width of the blade of the screwdriver against the slot in the head of the screw. If the blade is too small, the screw will twist or chip. You may even damage the screw head so much so that you may not be able to unscrew it. If the blade is too large it will continue to slip out as you try and fix the screw, and if the sides of the blade overhang the screw head, it will start to damage the wood that surrounds the screw head.

FINISHING IT OFF – STEPS 21 TO 24

21 Secure the slat supports with glue and 2-inch No.8 screws. When they are all in place, lay four slats on each shelf. Place two slats against the front and back shelf support and the other two evenly spaced out between them. Glue each end of the slats in place and then fix with two 1-inch panel pins at each end of every shelf slat.

22 Sand down all the rough edges of the hallstand to remove any splinters, using medium then fine sandpaper. If you wish, cover the screws with wood-coloured filler.

23 If you wish, attach two wooden drawer pulls to the front posts of the stand, drilling small pilot holes into the wood if necessary. You may not need to drill pilot holes, depending on the type of drawer pull you use and if the screw is small enough.

24 Finally, sand the dried filler and any rough edges of the hallstand, paying particular attention to any pencil marks. Then paint the stand in clear satin varnish or in a woodstain.

POWER SANDERS

When it comes to sanding down a large piece of furniture such as this hallstand, you may want to use a power sander. Power sanders work by attaching a special abrasive paper to part of the sander that moves in a fast circular motion. For this reason, when sanding over large flat areas, you should always finish off sanding by hand, taking care to sand in the direction of the wood grain. Power sanders are available in a variety of sizes. If you are going to buy one, choose one that is most suitable for your requirements.

UNDERSTAIR TIDY

Make the most of space under the stairs with a purpose-built storage unit. This imaginative and good-looking design allows easy access – it is built on castors – and offers ample storage space for bulky items that won't fit elsewhere.

EQUIPMENT

Pencil

Bradawl

Jigsaw

Tape measure

Sandpaper
(medium and fine)

Power drill/
Screwdriver

No.5 drill bit

Electric sander
(optional)

Combination
square/
Angle finder

Ruler

Clamp

MATERIALS

❖ Sheet of ½-inch mdf, 4 by 12 feet (see tip box on page 29)

❖ No. 6 screws, 1¼ inch long

❖ Panel pins, 1 inch long

❖ Set of four castors, with screws

❖ Quick-drying wood-coloured filler (optional)

❖ Handle or drawer pull

VARIATION

❖ Beading or moulding, about 10 feet long

❖ Panel pins (the size depends on the thickness of the beading or moulding you choose)

❖ Quick-drying filler

❖ Matt varnish

❖ Wood glue

❖ Emulsion paint

❖ Handle or drawer pull

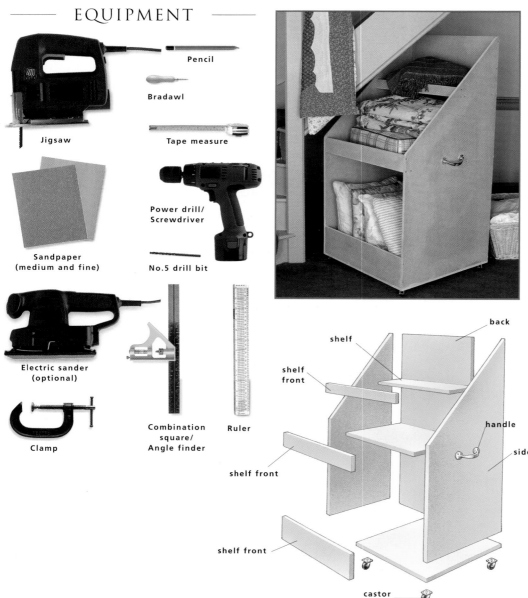

back

shelf

shelf
front

shelf front

handle

side piece

shelf front

castor

NOTE

Depending on individual circumstances, the height of the unit and the angle at the top will differ. The unit made for this project measures 48 inches at its highest point. If your unit needs to be higher than this, you will obviously need to buy more mdf, but when working out what height to make your understair tidy, always take into accout the height of the castors.

STARTING OUT - STEPS 1 TO 4

1 Measure and cut two pieces of mdf 24 by 48 inches for the sides of the cupboard. Then measure the angle under your stairs with an angle finder. On one of the short ends on each side piece, draw a line from one corner at the appropriate angle.

2 Lay one of the side pieces on a work bench and secure it in position. Using a jigsaw, carefully cut along the pencil line. Then do the same for the other side piece. On each side piece, draw a line ½ inch in from each of the straight sides.

3 Draw a line across the side piece where the shelves will go – ours were at 23, and 33 inches from the bottom. Then draw a line ½ inch above each line. Do the same on the other side piece. Mark where the shelf fronts will go (the middle shelf front was flush with the edge and 3 inches high; and the top shelf front was 9½ inches from the back and 2 inches high). Draw a ½-inch guideline next to these lines.

4 Cut a piece of mdf 25 by 48 inches. This is the back of the cupboard. Copy the same measurements for the shelf heights on to the back piece. Then add the ½ inch width in the same way. Hold the two sides and the back together and check that all the pencilled lines join up. If they don't, the shelves will be crooked, so take your time to measure and draw these carefully and accurately.

MEASURING AND MARKING

Mdf can be bought in large sheets, in some cases as large as eight feet long and four feet wide. When you are working with large sheets of mdf, it may be quite difficult for you to start measuring and marking up all the pieces you have to cut out. Instead, divide and cut the one large sheet into more manageable sizes, allowing about about ¹⁄₁₆ inch oversize before cutting. (On rough-sawn timber you should allow about 1 inch oversize.) Once cut into smaller sizes, you can then draw and cut out the rest of your pieces more accurately.

PUTTING IT TOGETHER – STEPS 5 TO 8

5 Cut out a piece of mdf 24 by 25 inches with a jigsaw. This piece is the base of the cupboard. Along each side, draw a line ½ inch in from edge. This border is where the sides and back will sit on the base.

6 Next, place a castor just in from the pencilled border at each corner. Mark where the screws go by placing a sharp pencil through each of the holes for screws in the base of the castor. Do the same for each corner but do not add the castors yet (see Step 15). Then, drill evenly-spaced pilot holes (about every 4 or 5 inches) within the pencilled border. Countersink each drilled hole.

7 Drill pilot holes for the shelves on the two side pieces and the back piece. These should be evenly spaced out, about 4 or 5 inches apart. Make sure they are within the pencilled ½-inch widths you made in Steps 2, 3 and 4. Turn the sides and the back piece over and countersink each hole.

8 You can now start to assemble the cupboard. Hold one side perpendicular to the back piece and screw the pieces together with a 1¼-inch screw in each pilot hole. (Ensure that when screwing the boards together the drawn lines face inward.) Attach the other side piece to the back in the same way.

ALL ABOUT CASTORS

Castors are simply small wheels that enable you to move pieces of furniture. They are easier to fit than ordinary wheels because they work individually, not in pairs, so an axle is not required. Depending on the size of the furniture and of the castor, there should be at least three castors under any piece of furniture for balance. Castors come in a range of shapes and sizes so get advice from your supplier if you are unsure of what you need. Some, for example, have a mounting plate while others screw directly into wood.

PUTTING IT TOGETHER - STEPS 9 TO 12

9 Lay the cupboard down on its back. Hold the base over the end and attach it by fixing screws through the pilot holes around the perimeter of the base. When drilling into a corner, be careful not to split the wood (see below).

10 On the remaining mdf mark up three pieces: measuring 6 by 25 inches, 3 by 25 inches and 2 by 25 inches. These three pieces are the fronts of the shelves. Then measure and mark up the shelves: measuring 9½ by 25 inches and 23½ by 24 inches. Cut out these five pieces with a jigsaw.

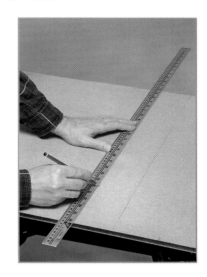

11 Hold the first shelf on the guidelines and check that the pilot holes are aligned with the shelf. Attach the shelf by fixing a screw in each pilot hole along the side pieces and through the back piece. Attach the second shelf in the same way. If you do not have someone at hand to help you hold the shelf in place, you may find it easier to finish assembling the cupboard on its back.

12 The fronts sit in front of, not on top of the shelves, since this gives a neater finish. Place some wood glue along the front of the shelf and then put the front piece in place so that the bottom edges align. Secure it with screws through the side and two panel pins through the front. Attach the middle front piece the same way. The lowest front piece sits on top of the base, so that it is flush with the sides.

PROFESSIONAL TIP

Mdf is made of compressed wood fibres bonded together. Due to the nature of its construction, you must take care when screwing close to an edge, as the wood has a tendency to split. To avoid this, drill your pilot holes about 1 inch away from any cut edge wherever possible. Otherwise, place your drill in the pilot hole and drill slightly into the next piece of wood. Then, when you fix the screw with your screwdriver, use a "pump action" to periodically ease off the pressure as you go. If the mdf splits, cover it with wood filler.

FINISHING IT OFF – STEPS 13 TO 16

13 Cut the pointed tips off at the top of the cupboard. If you have an electric sander, you can sand them down, but this creates a lot of dust. If you wish to paint the unit, cover all screws with filler and leave it to dry. Sand the cupboard thoroughly.

14 Paint with varnish or with whatever paint finish suits the area in which the storage unit is eventually to stand.

15 Add the four castors, screwing them in to place in the pilot holes. Make sure the screws are no longer than ½ inch. In order to avoid damage to stored items, make sure they do not penetrate the base of the unit.

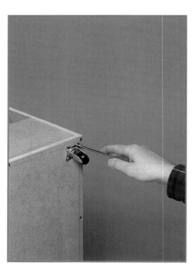

16 Finally, add the handle. If the screw is short, you may not have to drill a pilot hole, but remember to break the surface of the wood with a bradawl. Measure the width of the cupboard and place the handle in the centre, at a height that is easy for you to reach without having to bend over awkwardly.

MAKING A DOOR

If you wish to protect the contents of your understair cupboard, it is very easy to make a door for the lower shelf as all the sides are straight. Do not make the shelf front for the lowest shelf (shown in Step 10) and measure the area from the base to the bottom of the middle shelf. Cut out a piece of mdf to required size and fit the door with some hinges. Add a small piece of mdf just inside the shelf space to prevent the door swinging into the cupboard. For ideas about ways to keep the door closed, see the tip box on page 58.

VARIATION ~ MOULDED PANELS

1 Choose moulding or beading to suit the style of the stairs. Start by holding the beading 2½ inches from each edge and tracing its width in pencil. Make sure the beading is completely straight along the edge otherwise it will look crooked at a distance. Cut the beading strips slightly longer than necessary, as they will be cut again in Step 2.

2 To make mitred corners on the beading, hold one of the pieces of the beading on the pencilled guidelines so that it overlaps the adjacent set of guidelines. Mark the beading where it intersects the guidelines. Turn the beading over to its flat side and join up the two points. Continue in the same way for all the corners of beading and then cut all the mitres.

3 To fix the beading to the unit, put some wood glue on the back of a strip of beading and place it on the guideline. Secure the beading with evenly spaced panel pins. Continue until you have fixed all the beading to the cupboard. Use a nail punch to hide the heads of the panel pins.

4 If you are going to paint the cupboard, cover all the screws and the panel pins on the beading with quick-drying filler. Leave the filler to dry and then sand back. You can choose to paint the cupboard one colour, or you can paint the central panel another colour. Protect the paintwork with a coat of matt varnish. If you wish, you can add a handle or a drawer pull.

DECORATING YOUR PANEL

If you wish to add further decoration to the side of your understair cupboard, try filling in the space created by the moulding. For example, glue a decorative and colourful piece of fabric that has been cut to size to the cupboard, before adding the beading. Or make the framed space a decoupage feature or simply paint it in a contrasting colour. If you feel adventurous, try a special paint effect. Your local paint supply shop is sure to be stocked with a number of different ready-to-apply paint finishes.

DESKTOP ORGANISER

Say goodbye to clutter on your desktop with this handsome and practical organizer.
With a special compartment for your computer monitor, it also has adjustable
shelving so you can adapt it to meet your needs.

EQUIPMENT

No.5 drill bit

Countersink bit

Pencil

Jigsaw

Power drill/
Screwdriver

Paintbrush

Sandpaper
(medium and fine)

Combination square

Small bowl to use
as a palette

Ruler

Tenon saw

Clamp (optional)

Newspaper or dust sheet

MATERIALS

❖ Sheet of ½-inch mdf, 4 by 8 feet

❖ Length of doweling, 6 inches long and ¼ inch in diameter

❖ No. 6 screws, 1¾ inches long

❖ Matt varnish

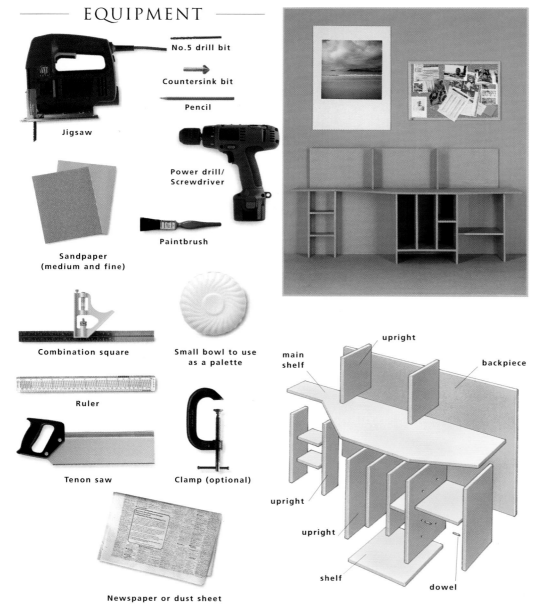

upright

main
shelf

backpiece

upright

upright

shelf

dowel

NOTE

This desktop organiser incorporates room for a computer monitor measuring 13 by 13½ inches. Measure your own monitor and change the layout guide to fit it if necessary. This will involve moving the uprights, which will not be a problem – but you will need to check the back piece when you drill pilot holes. If you need to raise the shelf, you will need to make adjustments to the cutting plan, because the uprights will be longer, although the shelf widths will remain the same.

STARTING OUT – STEPS 1 TO 4

1 Measure and cut out a piece of mdf, 27 inches by 48 inches long (see the cutting diagram on page 43), for the back piece. Measure and draw in the layout guide on page 43 in pencil. The horizontal guidelines represent the position of the shelves and the vertical guidelines represent the positions of all the vertical dividers.

2 The guidelines are drawn up to allow you to drill pilot holes in the correct place. Each set of guidelines represents the width of the wood that will be secured through the back piece, so you should drill pilot holes in the middle of the guidelines at regular intervals, about 4 to 5 inches apart.

3 Measure and mark out the main shelf on a piece of mdf, according to the cutting plan on page 43. Clamp the mdf securely and cut out the piece with a jigsaw.

4 The main shelf will rest on the upright dividers, so it is necessary to drill pilot holes through it to secure the uprights. To draw the guidelines, rest the main shelf on its guide-line on the back piece, marking the 4-inch overhang on each side. Then, extend all the lines onto the main shelf. For accuracy, first copy the lines onto the width of the mdf, and then extend them over the shelf.

BEFORE YOU START

The desktop organiser is not difficult to make but there are a few things to remember that will help make its construction easier. When you cut out all the pieces on the cutting plan on page 43, number each piece clearly in pencil. Also, mark the top and bottom of the uprights – this is important after you have marked pilot holes. And don't forget to check that all the sides are straight and square as you go. Before assembling the organiser, hold or "lean" everything in place, to check it for accuracy.

PUTTING IT TOGETHER – STEPS 5 TO 8

5 Drill pilot holes through the main shelf as you did in Step 2, in the middle of the guidelines and evenly spaced, about 4 or 5 inches apart. Remember, the shelf overhangs the uprights by about 1 inch so do not drill pilot holes closer than 1½ inches from the front edge of the shelf. Then, turn the mdf over and countersink each hole.

6 Measure and cut out all the upright dividers. On the diagram on page 42, these are pieces numbered 1, 2, 3, 4, 5, 6, 7, 8 and 9. You should have two pieces measuring 5 by 17 inches, two measuring 14 by 17 inches, two at 13½ by 14 inches, two at 6 by 10½ inches, and one piece measuring 11 by 17 inches. As you cut each piece out, number it in pencil to make the task of assembling the organiser easier.

7 Shelves 13 and 14 are adjustable and are held in place with small pieces of dowel. To mark the dowel rebates, draw a line 3¼ inches in from each 17-inch side of upright 7. Mark the side of upright 4 that faces toward upright 7 this way. On the side of upright 4 that faces upright 5, mark the rebates at 6 inches from each 17-inch edge. Repeat this measurement on upright 5 (see below).

8 Mark the dowel rebates on the lines you have just drawn. Make them about 5 inches apart, or customise the positions to suit your own needs. Use a combination square and a ruler to make sure that the rebates align. Drill the rebates so that they are ¼ inch deep. Use the depth gauge on your drill for this, or wrap some tape on the drill bit (see professional tip on page 89).

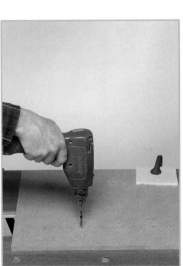

PROFESSIONAL TIP

When measuring and drilling the doweling rebates in Steps 7 and 8 make sure you mark in pencil which end is the top and bottom on each of the pieces. If you assemble your desktop organiser and place one of these uprights upside down, you may have to take it apart and reassemble a few pieces or you may even end up with holes in the wrong places. To avoid sloping shelves, check and then double check that the positions for the rebates align before drilling them.

PUTTING IT TOGETHER — STEPS 9 TO 12

9 Shelf number 12 is 3 inches up from the bottom of the organiser. To mark guides for pilot holes, draw lines 3 and 3½ inches in from one of the 14-inch sides on upright 3. Alternatively, place a piece of the mdf 3 inches in from one side and trace its width. Mark upright 4 in the same way, making sure you have checked which is the bottom end.

10 Mark in pencil evenly spaced pilot holes in the uprights 3 and 4. As before, they should be in the middle of the guidelines and about 4 or 5 inches apart. Turn the pieces over and countersink each hole.

11 Now measure and mark on the mdf all the shelves using the cutting plan on page 43 as a guide. The shelves are the pieces numbered 10, 11, 12, 13, 14. Once you have cut out these pieces with a jigsaw, check that you have one piece measuring 14 by 4½ inches, two pieces 5 by 6 inches, one piece measuring 13¾ by 14 inches and one 11 by 11¼ inches.

12 The shelf numbered 12 is fixed to the two uprights numbered 3 and 4 as well as to 6 and 7. You need to drill pilot holes through the shelf so that you can attach it to uprights 6 and 7. To mark where they go, draw a line 4¼ and 4¾ inches in from each 17-inch edge. Mark and drill pilot holes as before. Turn the piece over and countersink each hole.

PROFESSIONAL TIP

A jigsaw has a guide to help make a cut parallel to the edge of the wood, but only use it if the side of the wood is straight, the blade sharp and the wood is of a uniform consistency. The teeth point upward on a jigsaw blade, so the cleanest part of the cut will be underneath the wood. When using mdf, however, this is not a problem as mdf does not splinter. For safety's sake, take care to keep the power cord clear of the blade. Do not remove the saw from the wood until it has stopped moving.

FINISHING IT OFF – STEPS 13 TO 16

13 To assemble the organiser, find a flat surface to work on. Hold upright number 1 against the back piece on the guideline and secure it by driving a screw through the pilot holes on the back piece. Secure upright number 5 to the back piece in the same way. Make sure the dowel rebates are facing the right way.

14 Rest the main shelf on the two uprights already fixed in place. Check that the guidelines on the main shelf align with those on the back piece before fixing the shelf to the back piece and to uprights 1 and 5. Then fix the main shelf to uprights 2, 3 and 4 by screwing through the main shelf. Remember to fix uprights 2, 3 and 4 to the back piece too.

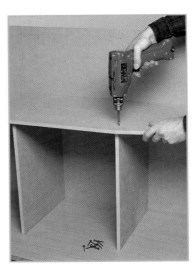

15 Lay the organiser on its back. Fix uprights 6 and 7 to the main shelf and then place shelf number 12 in position directly underneath them. Fix shelf 12 in position through pilot holes through uprights 3 and 4, and on to uprights 6 and 7 through the pilot holes in the shelf. Then add shelves 10 and 11 between uprights 1 and 2 in the same way.

16 Cut lengths of doweling to ½ inch lengths and place them in the rebates where you want shelves 13 and 14. Lift the organiser up and check for any unfilled pilot holes at the back. To finish off the organiser, sand and wipe it over with a damp cloth and paint on one or two coats of matt varnish, using newspaper or a dust sheet to protect your work surface.

FINISHING TOUCHES

If you prefer to conceal the screws, cover them with quick-drying filler and leave them to dry. This should take about 10 minutes, but always follow the manufacturer's instructions. You can then paint your desktop organiser any way you like – the same colour as your desk, or match the colour of the wall behind the desk. Once the surface of mdf is sealed with paint, you can embellish it with any kind of decorative effect you like, except wood staining. Consider using decoupage or perhaps stencilling.

DESKTOP ORGANISER DIAGRAM

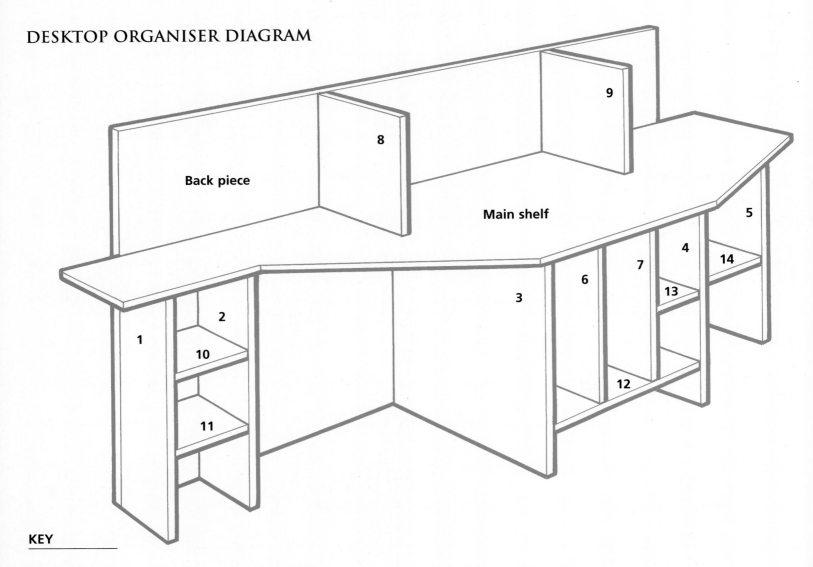

Back piece

Main shelf

KEY

1 - 5 x 17 inches

2 - 5 x 17 inches

3 - 14 x 17 inches

4 - 14 x 17 inches

5 - 11 x 17 inches

6 - 14 x 13½ inches

7 - 14 x 13½ inches

8 - 10½ x 6 inches

9 - 10½ x 6 inches

10 - 5 x 6 inches

11 - 5 x 6 inches

12 - 13¾ x 14 inches

13 - 14 x 4¼ inches

14 - 11¼ x 11 inches

Back piece - 28 x 48 inches

Main shelf - see cutting diagram

CUTTING DIAGRAM

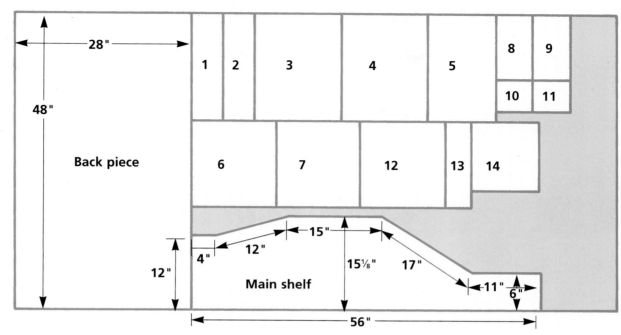

BACK PIECE LAYOUT DIAGRAM

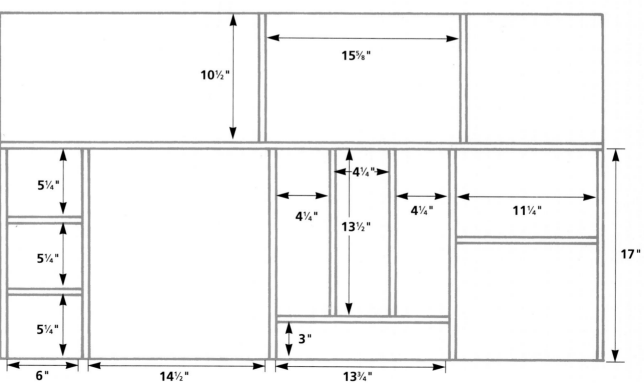

SHOE TIDY

This capacious yet space-saving organiser provides a neat and stylish solution to the perennial problem of storing shoes. Suspended in this dual-sided hanger, they are readily accessible while your wardrobe floor is freed of clutter.

EQUIPMENT

Iron

Scissors

Pencil or dressmaker's chalk

Ruler

Pins

Needle and thread

Sewing machine

Stitch tearer

MATERIALS

❖ Piece of deck-chair or other heavy canvas, at least 5 feet long and 15 inches wide

❖ Floral or other complementary fabric, 39 by 52 inches

❖ Binding, about 35 feet long, to complement floral fabric

❖ Velcro, 26 inches long, 1 inch wide

❖ Coat hanger

VARIATION

❖ Backing material, 7½ by 8 inches

❖ Piece of complementary fabric, 6 by 8 inches

❖ Binding, about 40 inches long

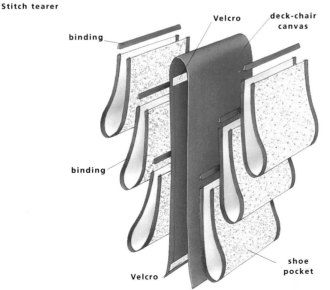

binding

Velcro

deck-chair canvas

binding

Velcro

shoe pocket

NOTE

If you want to make the extra pocket in the variation, remember that you need to sew it to the shoe pocket before you sew it to the central hanging piece.

STARTING OUT - STEPS 1 TO 4

1 If your canvas is not already cut to size, measure and mark out an area 15 by 60 inches and cut this out with scissors. Remember to make use of any selvedge edges, as these will help you keep your lines straight.

2 You need to press a 1-inch hem all around. If you are using deck-chair canvas, do not iron. Just fold over each edge and run a ruler along the crease – the material should stay folded. If you are using heavier canvas, you may need to iron it flat. To avoid bulky corners, measure 1 inch away from each corner and draw a diagonal from each point. Cut these corner pieces off.

3 Using a sewing machine, sew each 1-inch hem with zigzag stitch. Zigzag stitch is stronger than straight stitches and all the seams need to be secure. If you do not have a sewing machine, you could use carpet tape, which is a strong, double-sided adhesive tape. Ordinary double-sided tape is not strong enough, neither is hemming tape.

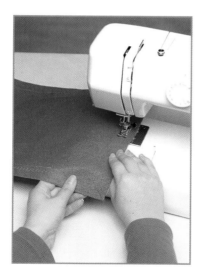

4 Lay the floral or complementary-coloured fabric out on your work surface. Measure and mark out six rectangles 13 inches wide and 26 inches long. Cut out each piece, taking care to keep the edges straight.

CHOOSING A SUITABLE FABRIC

The central section of the shoe tidy needs to be made from a much heavier-weight fabric than that used for the pockets. We used deck-chair canvas, which is heavy enough to carry the weight of the shoes and also comes in a good range of colours. If you do not use deck-chair material, you will need to find a very heavy-weight material of similar strength. Heavy-weight material is relatively thick, so you may need to make sure you have a suitable needle for your sewing machine.

PUTTING IT TOGETHER – STEPS 5 TO 8

5 Carefully fold the binding over in half and press a crease along it with an iron. You will need to press about 80 inches for each pocket.

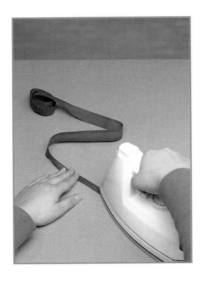

6 Place the binding so that the crease covers the edge of the fabric. Pin the binding down the two long sides of the piece. When you get to the end of one side, cut the binding and do the other side. Repeat for the other five pieces.

7 Stitch the binding to the piece of floral material with a sewing machine, removing the pins as you sew. The stitching will be much stronger and the task will be quicker than if you sew it by hand. Do the same for the other five pieces.

8 Fold one of the floral pieces in half so that the two "raw" edges meet. Then place a piece of binding on the edges, so that the crease of the binding covers the two edges. Pin the binding in place. Do the same for the other five pieces of floral material.

FITTING THE BINDING

Pressing the binding in half with an iron helps it to fit easily around the edges of the cut-out pocket pieces. Keep checking that the raw edge of the pocket fabric is pushed right into the fold of the binding as you pin it. When turning a corner of the pocket, the binding can be folded flat to give a neat mitred corner. When you pin the binding, remember to put the pins in the right direction so that you can remove them as you sew. If the pins are put in at a right angle to the stitching, they can be oversewn and removed afterward.

PUTTING IT TOGETHER – STEPS 9 TO 12

9 Thread a needle with a contrasting coloured thread. Use this to baste or tack the seam you have just pinned. Remove the pins as you sew. Do the same to the other five floral pockets.

10 Fold the piece of canvas in half with the right side facing out and make a crease. Make a mark 1½ inches down from this crease and close to each edge. Use a pencil or dressmaker's chalk to do this. Turn the canvas over and make a mark 1½ inches down on the other side of the crease.

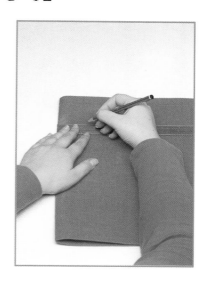

11 From the two sets of marks you have just made, make two more marks at 7-inch intervals on each side of the crease (you should end-up with a total of eight marks – four on each side of the canvas). Make sure you make the marks close to each edge, as this will help keep the pockets straight.

12 Pin each of the pockets to the marks you have made, making sure they are straight. The pockets should overlap each other and you should have three pockets on each side of the central crease.

BASTING

Although basting may seem like a step that could be omitted to save time, it really will help you achieve the neatest possible result. Use a brightly contrasting thread so the stitches are easy to see. Also, make the stitches large and widely spaced out, so that they will be easy to pull out when the machine-stitching is done. The main advantage of stitching over an already-basted seam is that you have the uninterrupted use of both hands to guide the fabric through the machine as you stitch it.

FINISHING IT OFF – STEPS 13 TO 16

13 Stitch each floral pocket to the canvas, using zigzag stitch for added strength. Start at one end, and as you do each pocket, roll up the ones you have already done so they fit through the sewing machine. Remove the pins as you go and when you have sewn all the pockets, remove the basting with a stitch tearer.

14 Lay the shoe tidy out on your work surface, right side down. Measure and cut a 13-inch length of Velcro. Attach the Velcro 1 inch on either side of this central crease.

15 Measure out another 13-inch length of Velcro and attach this to each end of the canvas.

16 To hang up the shoe tidy, thread a sturdy coat hanger through the canvas, so that the central crease rests on the hanger. Press together the lengths of Velcro at the top and bottom of the shoe tidy. You can then hang it up in a wardrobe or hall cupboard, storing shoes in each of the shoe pockets.

VELCRO

Velcro, a invaluable invention with a variety of uses, comes in many different strengths, from the heavy-duty to the light-weight. It also comes in a range of widths, including small individual Velcro dots. Some Velcro has an adhesive backing, like the one we used in this project. This means you can stick pieces of Velcro down without pinning, basting or sewing it into place. This type of Velcro is slightly more expensive than ordinary Velcro, which does require sewing.

VARIATION - EXTRA POCKETS

1 To make an extra pocket for polish, a shoe horn or a suede brush, cut out a piece of backing material 6 by 8 inches and a piece of material for the front measuring 7½ by 8 inches. Iron about 40 inches of bias binding in half, as before. Pin the binding over one long side of the front material and sew it into place on a sewing machine.

2 Then hold the front piece against the backing material and pin binding around the perimeter of the pocket. Then stitch around the whole pocket to join the two pieces together.

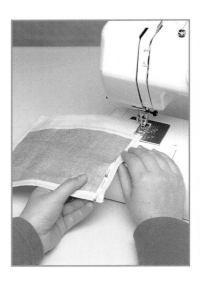

3 To make individual pockets, divide the pocket equally into three, or make sections of unequal sizes to suit the proposed contents of the pockets. Mark each division with a pin and stitch it, removing the pins as you go.

4 Finally, sew the pocket on to the shoe pocket, before you sew it on to the main piece of canvas. The extra pocket should be positioned about 1 inch down from the top edge and pinned into place before you stitch it.

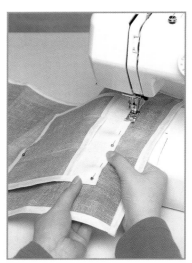

CUSTOM-MADE EXTRAS

This extra version of the shoe tidy is made from a natural fabric called linen scrim, which looks as rough and rustic as hessian but is quite a soft material by comparison. The backing material on the extra pocket is unbleached calico. The two materials show how the shoe tidy can have a completely different look. The extra pocket can be customized to fit your personal requirements, so make sure you measure any polish, shoehorns or brushes you have and then divide up your compartments accordingly.

PICTURE BOX CUPBOARD

There is no need to buy a new picture frame to make this cupboard. You can use an old junk-shop find, or use a picture you like already hanging in your house. Simply make it more practical by building a cupboard behind it.

EQUIPMENT

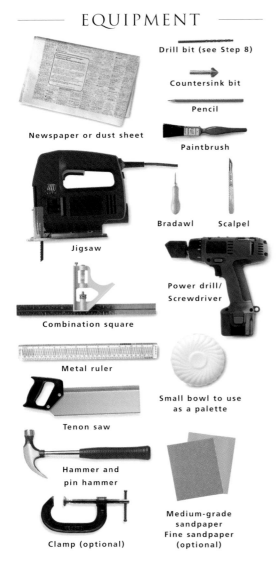

Drill bit (see Step 8)

Countersink bit

Pencil

Newspaper or dust sheet

Paintbrush

Jigsaw

Bradawl   **Scalpel**

Power drill/
Screwdriver

Combination square

Metal ruler

Small bowl to use
as a palette

Tenon saw

Hammer and
pin hammer

Clamp (optional)

Medium-grade
sandpaper
Fine sandpaper
(optional)

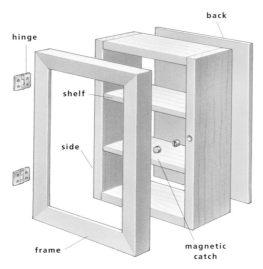

hinge

back

shelf

side

frame

magnetic
catch

MATERIALS

To make a cupboard 13 by 10¾ by 5¼ inches:

❖ Picture frame 13 by 10¾ inches (see note)

❖ Sheet of ½-inch mdf about 11 by 13 inches,

❖ Piece of pine 4 by ½ inch, 4 feet long, for the box

❖ Piece of pine, 3½ by ¼-inch 19 inches long, for the shelves

❖ 1-inch nails

❖ Quick-drying filler

❖ Picture for the frame and paper glue or spray adhesive

❖ Spirit level (optional)

VARIATION

❖ Pine and mdf (see below)

❖ 1-inch panel pins

❖ Quick-drying filler

❖ Mug hooks, to hold keys

❖ Emulsion paint

❖ Catch (see page 58)

NOTE

Depending on the size of your frame you will need to adjust the amount of mdf and pine you need. For amount of mdf, measure the length and height of the frame and multiply the figures together. Measure each side and add the figures together for how much pine you need for the box. Multiply the width by the number of shelves for how much pine you need for the shelves.

STARTING OUT – STEPS 1 TO 4

1 To make the back of the cupboard, place the picture frame on the sheet of mdf and trace around it in pencil. This is more accurate than measuring the length of each side and making each corner square. Make use of its straight sides by placing the frame in the corner of the mdf. You then only have to make two cuts. To make the shelves, measure two lengths of 9¾ inches on the thinner pine and cut these out with a jigsaw (see below).

2 Measure two lengths of pine of 9¾ inches and two lengths of 13 inches. If the frame you are using is a different size, measure each side and transfer these measurements to the length of pine (see below). Use a combination square to draw straight lines at these points, then cut the lengths with a jigsaw. These four lengths of wood are the sides of the box.

3 Attach the four sides together to make a box, applying wood glue and three nails to each join. Place the shorter sides between the longer ones so that the joins will be at the top and bottom of the cupboard, not at the side, where they would be visible.

4 Using a combination square, check that all the sides are straight. Place the back of the cupboard over the sides. Check again that everything is straight. Hold the back in place by hammering in nails about 3 inches apart and in every corner. Make sure that the nails are within ½ inch from the edge, to allow for the thickness of the wood.

PROFESSIONAL TIP

If you are making a box for a frame smaller or larger than the one used in this project, you need to measure the sides yourself. However, when doing so, you must remember to allow for the thickness of the wood on two of the sides. For example, if the top piece fits between the two side pieces of wood, you need to subtract 1 inch (two times the thickness of the wood) from the length. The length of the shelves is the width of the frame minus two times the thickness of the wood.

PUTTING IT TOGETHER – STEPS 5 TO 8

5 Turn the box on its side and measure and mark 4 inches and 8 inches from the top, for the shelves. (If your cupboard is a different size, you will have to decide where to place the shelves.) Use a combination square to draw lines at these points, then do the same on the other side of the box. Stand the box upright and check that the pencil marks are exact. (You may want to use a spirit level here.)

6 Decide whether you will place the shelves above or below the lines you marked. Put some wood glue on either end of the shelf and place it in position. Secure the shelf with three evenly spaced panel pins. Check that the shelf is straight and then hammer in three panel pins on the other side. Wipe away any excess wood glue and punch the pin heads into the wood. Attach the other shelf in the same way.

7 Cover all nails and panel pins with quick-drying filler. If you do not intend to paint the cupboard, use a wood-coloured filler. Leave the filler to dry. (This should take about 10 minutes, but follow the manufacturer's instructions.) Sand all the edges of the cupboard. For a smooth finish, use coarse sandpaper first and then finish with fine sandpaper.

8 Locate the midpoint of the front edge of the box on the right side and make a pencil mark for the magnetic catch. Drill a hole on the mark using a drill bit suitable for the size of catch you have. To mark the depth of the hole, flag the drill bit with tape. When the tape touches the wood, it is the right depth. Do not insert the catch yet.

PROFESSIONAL TIP

When making shelves or any other type of wood work that needs fitting together, always cut your wood on the waste wood side of the line you have drawn. This means the piece of wood should be slightly larger than the size you actually need. Before gluing and nailing your pieces together, check how the pieces fit. Pieces of wood should fit quite snugly. If the fit is too tight, sand away the edges for a better fit. If the fit is too loose, you will have to cut another piece – or sand down all the other pieces!

PUTTING IT TOGETHER - STEPS 9 TO 12

9 If the cupboard is not the same colour as the frame, you can paint it. We painted the frame and the cupboard the same colour to contrast with the wall, but you could use a different colour for the frame and the cupboard, or use a colour that complements your wall colour. Leave the paint to dry, and if necessary, paint a second coat.

10 Holding the frame and the cupboard together, place the hinges on the side so that one half is on the cupboard and the other half is on the frame. Make sure the hinges are evenly spaced along the side. (We placed the hinges 2½ inches from each end.) Use a bradawl to break the surface of the wood through each hole in the hinges.

11 The size of the hinges you use will depend on the size of the frame you are using. Generally, if you use small hinges, you will be able to turn the screws directly into the wood, after breaking the surface with the bradawl. For a large frame using large hinges you may need to drill small pilot holes at each of the bradawl marks.

12 Insert the magnetic catch into the hole you drilled in the cupboard in Step 8. To place the other half of the catch accurately in the frame, place the other half of the magnetic catch on the half in the cupboard. Close the frame and the catch will mark it where it should be placed. Then gently hammer the catch into the frame. Place something under the frame to protect it while you hammer.

CHOOSING HINGES

There are many different types of hinge to choose from, from a concealed hinge that fits on the inside of the door to a barrel hinge, which allows the door to be removed from the cupboard without taking off the hinge. Use two hinges to keep the door of the cupboard stable. For large doors, you will need to buy a longer hinge, but the longer the hinge, the wider it is. You will need to check its width – the width of the hinge cannot be wider than the wood of the frame or the cupboard.

FINISHING IT OFF – STEPS 13 TO 16

13 If you are adding a new picture to the frame, cut this to fit. Use a sharp scalpel and a metal ruler for this task, as they will make a clean cut. If you want to use a mount, you need to decide whether the picture should go behind or in front of the mount.

14 Place the picture or pictures on a piece of backing paper. This is important if the picture is on thin paper. Secure the picture with paper glue or spray adhesive.

15 Place the glass in the picture frame, along with the picture and any mount or backing sheet, then the hard backing. Place the frame clips between the frame and the hard backing, at regular intervals around the perimeter. Take note when you remove the clips how to put them back in again, as there are a number of different types.

16 To attach the cupboard to a wall, you will need to drill one or two holes (depending on the size of the cupboard) through the back of the cupboard. Position the pilot holes near the top of the cupboard using a drill bit to suit the size screws you need for your wall. Once you have drilled the holes, countersink each one.

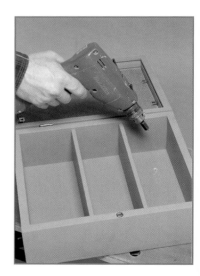

FILLING YOUR FRAME

You don't have to put expensive period prints or paintings in your frame. For an inexpensive alternative, try photocopying an interesting architectural detail or gothic gargoyle, or you could hand-colour a photocopy of an old botanical print or family photograph. For a more modern approach, cut out some pictures from magazines and make a collage, or frame your favourite photograph of a peaceful garden. You could frame a child's drawing for a more personalized cupboard.

VARIATION - KEY CUPBOARD

1 To make a cupboard for keys, find a frame that is a suitable size for the number of keys you have. Cut out the four sides and a back as before, and make a box following instructions on page 53, but do not cut out any shelves. When you have made the box, drill a hole for the catch if you are using one (see below) and paint the box if you wish.

2 Work out how many keys you have to put in the cupboard. Mark in pencil where each hook will go, then check that you will have enough room for the keys between each hook. When you are happy with your arrangement, break the surface of the wood at each point with a bradawl. Then screw in the mug hooks.

3 Place the frame and cupboard on its side and space out the hinges so that half of the hinge is on the frame and the other half is on the cupboard. Break the surface wood by placing a bradawl through each hole in the hinges and then screw the hinges into place. If the hinges and the screws are large, you may have to drill pilot holes for the screws first.

4 Finally, replace the picture, the mount if there is one, and the backing. Place the frame clips in the back of the frame at regular intervals to keep the picture in place. Fix the cupboard to the wall following instructions on page 56.

KEEPING YOUR CUPBOARD CLOSED

If your picture frame cupboard is quite small, it will probably not be necessary to attach any kind of catch in order to keep it closed, since the frame should not swing open. However, if the cupboard is, say, larger than about 5 by 7 inches, you will have to keep it closed in some way. The advantage of a magnetic catch is that it is unobtrusive, but there are several other options available. These include a hook and catch, a push-sensitive catch or, if the contents of the cupboard are private, lock and key.

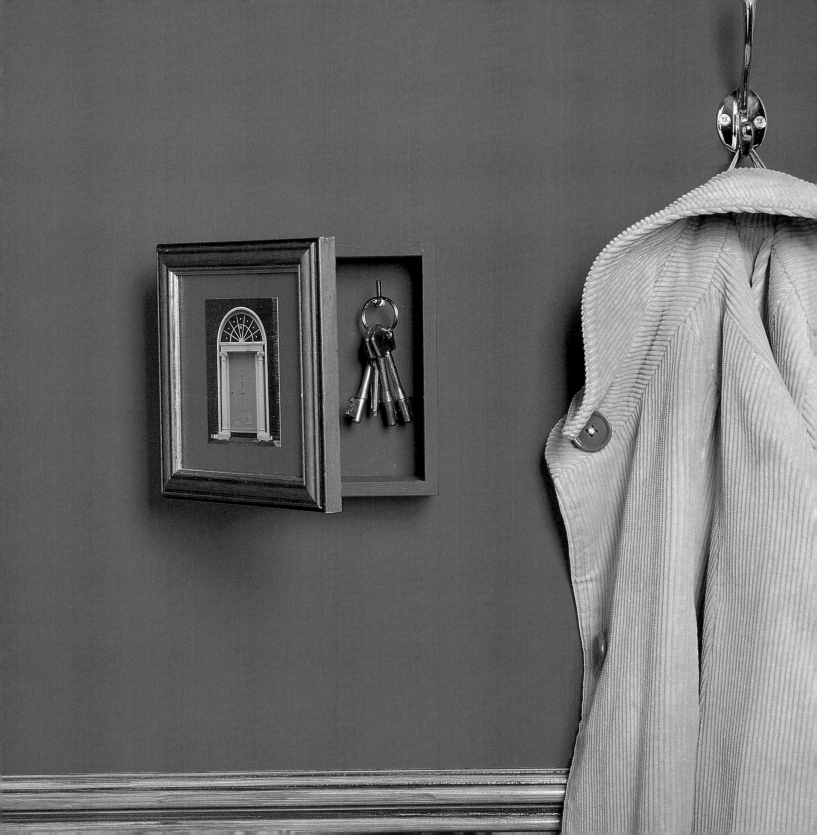

BATHROOM BOOKCASE

Lotions and potions, bottles and brushes, as well as the obligatory bathroom reading can all can be stored in this neat unit that puts to work a space too often neglected. Keep a simple pine finish or go for a distressed-paint effect.

EQUIPMENT

Pencil

Paintbrush

Jigsaw

Power drill/ Screwdriver

Combination square

Ruler

Hammer

Sandpaper (coarse, medium and fine)

Pin hammer

No.5 drill bit

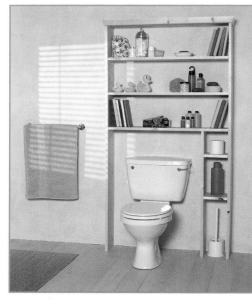

MATERIALS

To make a bookcase 38 by 72 inches:

❖ Five 6-foot lengths of pine, 7½ by ¾ inches

❖ Batten, 2 by 1 inch, 38 inches long

❖ Panel pins, 1 inch long

❖ No. 6 screws, 2 inches long

❖ Quick-drying wood-coloured filler

❖ Architrave, 5 feet long

VARIATION

❖ White emulsion paint

❖ Light blue emulsion pain

❖ Dark blue emulsion paint

❖ Paint kettle or small bucket for mixing paint

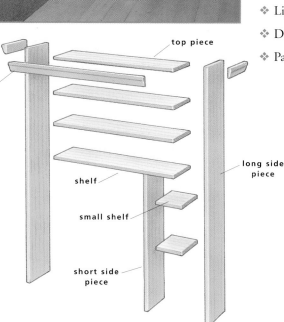

top piece

architrave

shelf

small shelf

short side piece

long side piece

STARTING OUT — STEPS 1 TO 4

1 Set aside two 72-inch lengths of pine for the long side pieces. Then cut one top piece at 38 inches, three shelves at 36½ inches and one short side piece at 39⅜ inches and two small shelves at 7 inches. Use a combination square to draw straight lines across the pine at these points. Then clamp the wood to your workbench or work surface and cut out each length with a jigsaw.

2 Decide which end of the the long 72-inch side pieces will be the top end and measure and mark the points at 10, 10¾, 21, 21¾, 32 and 32¾ inches from the "top" (see below). Mark the other long side piece the same way, but also mark lines at 39⅜ and 52⅝ inches.

3 Use a combination square to draw a straight line at all the points you marked in Step 2. Within each pair of these guidelines, mark three pilot holes but make sure the end ones are about 2 inches in from each edge.

4 On the piece of wood that is the top of the bookcase, place an offcut of wood on one end and trace its width. Place the offcut on the other end of the wood and mark it in the same way. Then mark a pilot hole 2 inches in from each edge and one in the centre of these, within each of these widths.

DRAWING UP GUIDELINES

There are two ways to measure up guidelines for pilot holes. The first, described in Step 2, involves measuring and marking where the bottom and top of the shelf will go. For example, if the wood is ¾ inch thick, mark 10 inches and then 10¾ inches. Another way to draw up guidelines is to mark a line where you want the shelves to go, and then place a width of pine on the line and trace its width. This method saves measuring, but you must remember to always place the width of wood on the same side of the line.

PUTTING IT TOGETHER - STEPS 5 TO 8

5 Decide which of the shelves will be the lowest. On this shelf, measure 7 and 7¾ inches in from one side and draw a straight line across the wood at this point with a combination square. Otherwise, place an offcut of wood on the line at 7 inches and trace its width as in Step 3. Then, mark a pilot hole 2 inches in from each edge and one in the centre, within this width.

6 Measure the position of the shelves on the short side piece. These are 8 inches and 20 inches from the top end of the piece. Mark the width of an offcut of wood as before, then measure and mark pilot holes, 2 inches in from each end and one in the centre, within each of the traced widths.

7 Before drilling pilot holes make sure that all the guidelines align. Then drill all the pilot holes you marked in Steps 2 to 6, using a No.5 drill bit. Then turn the wood over and countersink each of the holes.

8 You can now start to assemble the bookcase. Remember to secure each join with wood glue as well as screws. Hold the top piece to one of the sides and hold firmly while you fix the two pieces together with a screw in each pilot hole. Then add the other side piece in the same way (see below).

TAKING CARE

Although the bookcase looks easy to assemble, you must be careful not to make silly mistakes, such as drilling pilot holes in the wrong end of a length of wood. To avoid possible confusion it is worth numbering or labelling each piece of wood as you cut it out. In Step 8, make sure that both lengths of wood are the right way around by checking that the pilot holes for the shelves align before adding the top. Always check your work as you go and you should have no trouble assembling the bookcase.

PUTTING IT TOGETHER – STEPS 9 TO 12

9 Next, add the short side piece to the lowest shelf. Use a combination square to make sure the wood is screwed in straight. Use wood glue and a screw in each of the pilot holes you marked in Step 5.

10 Now join the short side and the lowest shelf to the frame you made in Step 8. Use glue and screws to fix the lowest shelf, adding the screws to the pilot holes at 32 inches from the top.

11 Next, add the two other shelves in the same way. Always use the combination square to ensure the shelves are square. If the shelves are slightly out, they can be nudged into shape.

12 Finally, add the last two small shelves at the pilot holes marked at 39⅝ and 52⅝ inches. Remember to glue all the joins as well as screw them together and keep them square with the combination square.

PROFESSIONAL TIP

When assembling this bookcase, your most trusted friend is the combination square. Without it, you will find it difficult to keep your shelves straight and square. A combination square does more than keep your drawn lines straight. If you set the combination square at a 45° angle, it can mark a mitre; and most combination squares come with a small level to check both horizontal and vertical levels. Most importantly, use it to check the squareness of all the joins in the bookcase, either on the outside or the inside of the corners.

FINISHING IT OFF – STEPS 13 TO 16

13 To keep the shelves square while the wood glue dries and also to keep the shelves together while you move the bookcase into place, attach a length of batten to the base with a nail at each end. There is no need to hammer the nail all the way into the wood. When the batten is just attached, hammer the nail so that it bends over as a safety precaution.

14 To add the architrave to the top of the shelves, measure and cut the architrave to the correct lengths using a combination square to mark the mitres (see tip on page 63) or with a mitre saw. Fix the architrave in place with glue and evenly spaced panel pins.

15 Sand down all the rough edges of the bookcase. Take your time doing this, as it will avoid splintering later. Start with coarse sandpaper first and then finish off with fine sandpaper. If you are short of time, you can use an electric sander.

16 If you wish, you can cover all the screws with wood-coloured filler and leave them to dry. If you use quick-drying filler it should dry in about 10 minutes (but always follow manufacturer's instructions). Protect the wood with one or two coats of clear satin varnish. When you are ready to put the bookcase in its place, remove the batten.

ARCHITRAVES

Don't be limited by a traditional-looking architrave. Depending on the style of your bathroom, you can choose any moulding or beading in any design that takes your fancy. Moulding comes in a whole variety of styles, ranging from geometric art deco styles to those with a range of fancy curves. If you chose a plain one, you can always stencil a pattern around the architrave – there is an abundance of ready-made stencils to choose from – or stamp on a design with a rubber stamp.

VARIATION - ANTIQUE PAINT EFFECT

1 Mix some white emulsion paint with enough water to give it the consistency of thin cream. Make sure you mix up enough paint to cover the entire bookcase. When you brush on the paint, you should be able to see the wood grain underneath.

2 When the white paint has dried, mix some light blue paint and water in the same way. When you paint the bookcase, you should be able to see white paint showing through. Leave the paint to dry.

3 When the light blue paint has dried, rub over the whole bookcase with sandpaper. Be careful not to take both coats of paint off.

4 Finally, dilute some dark blue paint as before and paint the bookcase. Leave the paint to dry and then lightly rub over the bookcase with sandpaper to complete the distressed effect.

PROFESSIONAL TIP

Diluting emulsion paint, or buying a special colourwash paint, adds colour to your bookcase without losing any of the natural grain of the timber. Pale colours, such as soft blue, muted green, white and pink do well with the pale, natural colour of pine. Whichever colour you choose, remember that it will look less strong once it has been diluted. Seal the wood against the humidity of the bathroom with a coat of varnish. To stop the varnish from changing the colour of the paint, use sanding sealer first.

HIDE-AWAY CARTS

Say goodbye to untidy bedrooms when you build these colourful underbed carts to house your children's clutter. Roll them out in the morning and back again – fully charged – at night, leaving the floor space delightfully free!

EQUIPMENT

Pencil

Paintbrush

No.5 drill bit

Jigsaw

Combination square

Sandpaper and sanding block

Ruler

Pin hammer

Clamp

Junior hacksaw

Power drill/ Screwdriver

NOTE

Wheels are available from hobby shops and come in a range of colours and sizes. If the carts are going underneath a bed, measure the distance between the floor and the bed before deciding what size wheels you buy. The wheels used here were 4 inches in diameter. Axles, fixing blocks and wheel ends also come in different sizes so you should be able to find components to fit the wheels in the one shop.

tear drop slot

side

rope

toggle

base

fixing block

washer

wheel

axle

wheel end

MATERIALS

To make one cart:

❖ Piece of pine, 7 by ¾ inches, 6½ feet long

❖ Piece of ¼-inch mdf or plywood, 15 inches by 2 feet

❖ 4 fixing blocks (see Step 11) and screws

❖ 4 wheels and wheel ends

❖ 4 washers

❖ Length of axle, 20 inches long, ¼ inch in diameter

❖ No. 6 screws, 2 inches long

❖ Quick-drying filler

❖ Emulsion paint (see Step 9) and newspaper or dust sheet to protect your work surface

❖ Scrap of wood, for clamping (see Step 3)

❖ Panel pins, ¾ inch long

❖ Wood glue

❖ Rope or cord, about 22 inches long, ½ inch thick (see Step 2) and sharp utility knife

❖ Toggle or piece of dowel, 4 inches long and ¾ inch in diameter, to use as a handle

VARIATION

To make one cover:

❖ Piece of strong, heavy fabric 17 by 26 inches

❖ Hemming tape and iron

❖ Velcro, 6 inches long, ¾ inch wide (see page 72 Step 4)

STARTING OUT – STEPS 1 TO 4

1 On the length of pine, measure out two lengths at 22½ inches and two lengths at 15 inches. Use a combination square to make sure the cutting lines you draw are at right angles to the edge of the wood. Then, cut out these four lengths of wood, which will form the sides of the cart.

2 Measure and mark the slots on the two 15-inch lengths. Mark the midpoint on one of the long sides and use a combination square to draw a 2-inch line at this point. Mark ⅛ inch on either side of the line at the top (the edge) and ¼ inch on either side at the bottom. Join up these points and round the bottom to form a "tear-drop" shape (see below).

3 Working on one of the lengths at a time, place the wood on a workbench and clamp it to make it secure. Then cut out the tear-drop shape. To do this easily, cut down the sides of the shape first and turn the jigsaw gradually into the wood to saw away the bottom of the tear-drop. When aiming for a snug fit, it is better to undercut, as you can always sand away the wood.

4 When you have cut out both tear-drop shapes, you need to drill pilot holes in each corner (on both pieces of wood). Using a No.5 drill bit, make these holes 1 inch in from each long edge. Because the wood you are joining is ¾ inch thick, make sure the holes are about ⅜ inch in from the short edges of the wood.

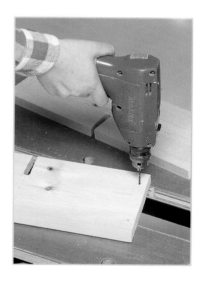

PROFESSIONAL TIP

When you come to measure and mark up the wedge-shape on the wood, you need to check its width against the thickness of the rope you have. If your rope is not ½ inch thick, you will have to change the measurements given in Step 2, above, so that the slot will be wide enough to take the width of your rope. Remember that the wedge-shape that you cut out should also be narrow enough to fit snugly. If you are unsure about the size, always undercut, you can always cut away some more until it fits.

PUTTING IT TOGETHER - STEPS 5 TO 8

5 Hold one of the 15-inch lengths and one of the 22½-inch lengths at right angles and glue the two pieces together. Secure them with a 2-inch screw in each pilot hole. Attach the other 22½-inch length in the same way, then add the other 15-inch length, making sure that the cut-out wedge shape is facing the same way (see below).

6 Place the sides of the cart on the sheet of mdf or plywood. Carefully trace around it in pencil. Then cut out this piece (the base) with a jigsaw, remembering to cut on the waste side of the wood.

7 Place the sides of the cart on your work surface so that the cut out tear-drop shapes are down. Place the base over the four sides and glue it into place with wood adhesive. Secure the base by hammering in ¾-inch panel pins, placed at 4-inch intervals around the perimeter of the base. Take care to hammer within ¾ inch from the edge, which is the thickness of the sides of the cart.

8 Cover all the screws with filler. Leave the filler to dry, which should take about 10 minutes (but always check the manufacturer's instructions); then sand all the edges of the cart. To sand inside the tear-drop shapes, roll a piece of sandpaper around a small object, such as a pencil and rub the sandpaper inside the cut edges.

KEEPING THE SIDES SQUARE

When you join the sides together in Step 5, make sure you check that each piece of wood is straight and that each corner is square before joining two pieces together. Check all the corners with a combination square as you go. When you have put the four sides together, if the box you have made isn't square, you can still straighten up the sides by pushing them gently. It is very important to remember to do this before you trace around the sides onto the mdf in Step 6, otherwise the base will be crooked too.

PUTTING IT TOGETHER – STEPS 9 TO 12

9 Protect your work surface with an old sheet or newspaper and paint the inside and outside of the cart in emulsion paint. Choose a colour to complement the colour of the room. If you are making several carts, choose different colours, or paint them one colour and use different colour lengths of cord to join them.

10 To make up the wheels, you need to cut the axle to the correct size. This will depend on the width of the wheels you have. Turn the cart over, with the base uppermost. To the width of the cart (15 inches) add the width of two wheels and then add 1 inch. Cut the axle to this length.

11 The fixing blocks you buy will probably have two holes in them already, for attaching them to your cart, but may not have a hole for your axle. If necessary, drill a hole on the side adjacent to the side with the two holes. But make sure the hole you drill allows for a snug fit as the axle should not move in the fixing block.

12 Each cart needs two pairs of wheels. To assemble each pair, first place the fixing block onto the axle. Then place a washer, a wheel and a wheel end onto the axle. Thread a fixing block, washer, wheel and wheel end onto the other side of the end of the axle. If you have made more than one cart, make more pairs of wheels as necessary.

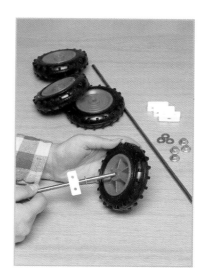

PROFESSIONAL TIP

If you think something is too difficult or complicated to attempt, read over the instructions several times, it may not be as difficult as it looks – or think of a simple alternative. For example, if you cannot find any wheels in your local hobby shop, or even if you think they are too difficult to attach to the cart, you could place four casters under the cart instead – one in each corner. Also, if you don't feel confident enough to use a jigsaw to cut out the tear-drop shape for the rope in Step 3, skip the step and add a drawer pull instead.

FINISHING IT OFF – STEPS 13 TO 16

13 You can now attach two pairs of wheels to the base of each cart. Measure 3 inches in from each short side of the box and place the wheels in position. Place a bradawl through the holes in the fixing block and break the surface of the base. Then secure the fixing block in place with screws (fixing blocks are usually sold with screws).

14 If you have made just one cart, you can now make the handle (see Step 16); if you have more than one, you will need to make a link as well. Cut the rope into required lengths: about 14 inches for a handle and 8 inches for a link. To prevent the rope fraying, wrap some tape around the end, then cut through the tape and the rope for a neat finish. If your rope is thick, you may need to cut it with a utility knife.

15 To make the links, tie a knot in each end of the 8-inch lengths. If you wish, you can trim the ends further by cutting through the tape and the rope with a utility knife. Make sure you do not cut too close to the knot, or it will come undone. Place the ends into the cut-out slots of two carts.

16 To make the handle, knot the ends of the 14-inch length of rope and place one end in the tear-drop shape. Thread the other end through the toggle and knot as before. If you don't have a toggle, use a piece of dowel, but you will need to drill a hole large enough to thread the rope through (see below).

PROFESSIONAL TIP

When drilling holes in a piece of dowel or any kind of circular piece of wood, take extra care that the wood doesn't slip. Use a vice or G-clamp to hold the wood securely – if the drill slips, your doweling will be ruined. However, even if you are an experienced woodworker and fairly confident using a power drill, you should always use a bradawl or nail to break the surface of the wood before you start drilling as this will help anchor the drill bit in the wood. Begin your drilling slowly, and then increase your speed.

VARIATION ~ MAKING A COVER

1 Make a cover for each of your storage carts to protect clothes or other items from dust. The cart should measure 15 by 24 inches, but measure the one you have made for accuracy. Then measure and cut out a piece of material measuring 17 by 26 inches, which allows for 1-inch hems.

2 You need to trim off the excess material at each corner. To do this neatly, mark a point 1 inch on either side of a corner. Extend lines at these points so that you have a 1-inch square where the two lines meet. Then, mark points 2 inches on either side of the corner. Place your ruler on these points and check that it touches the 1-inch square. Draw a line between the points and cut away the material. Repeat on each corner.

3 To make a hem, cut the hemming tape to the exact lengths of your cover. Lay the material on an ironing board wrong side up. Place a length of tape on one of the sides and press with a hot iron (always check manufacturer's instructions). Then turn the hem over and press again, until the hem is secure. Do the same for each side of the cover.

4 Attach your cover to the cart with Velcro. Cut four 1½-inch pieces of Velcro and place one half of each piece on the four corners of the cover. Place the other half on the four corners of the cart. You will need adhesive Velcro for this, or you will have to attach each piece to the cart with another type of adhesive, such as strong glue or carpet tape.

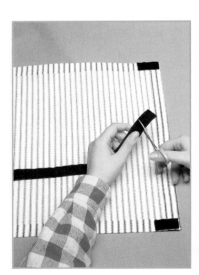

ALTERNATIVE FASTENERS

Making the cover that just reaches the ends of the cart means that you do not have to have know how to sew or how to use a sewing machine. However, there are alternatives to the simple cover shown above. For example, you could make a hemmed rectangle, 6 inches longer and wider than the cart and punch eyelets along the edges, or just one or two in the centre of each side. Make loops out of elastic and thread one through each eyelet. Screw some small hooks into the side of the cart to hold the elastic loops.

CHILD'S BOX SEAT

Kids will love this colourful two-seater bench, complete with room underneath for tidying away games and toys. Paint a farm scene or roads for toy cars on the seat, and when play time is over, cover the seat with its own cushion.

EQUIPMENT

Combination square (with level)

Ruler

Power drill/Screwdriver

Clamp

T-rule

Countersink bit   No.5 drill bit

Jigsaw   Paintbrush   Pencil

Bradawl

MATERIALS

❖ Piece of ¾-inch mdf, 4 by 6 feet

❖ Batten, 2 by 1 inches, 5½ feet long

❖ No. 6 screws, 1¾ and 1¼ inches long

❖ Two sets of hinges, about 1 inch long

❖ Panel pins, 1½ inches long

❖ Screws, 1½ inches long

❖ Wood glue

❖ Quick-drying filler and sandpaper

❖ Emulsion or acrylic paint (see Step 18)

❖ Satin or matt varnish

VARIATION

❖ Foam for cushion, about 14 by 36 inches, and sharp utility knife

❖ Piece of fabric, 33 by 41 inches

❖ Sewing machine or hemming tape

❖ Velcro, 15 inches long, 1 inch wide

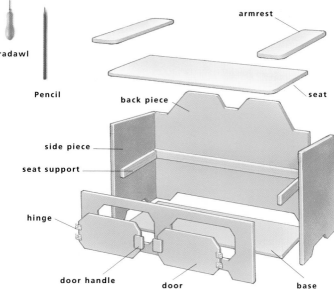

armrest

back piece

seat

side piece

seat support

hinge

door handle

door

base

STARTING OUT – STEPS 1 TO 4

1 Using a pencil and a T-rule, copy the cutting diagram on page 78 onto the sheet of mdf. (It may be easier to cut the mdf in thirds first, or ask your timber merchant to do this for you.) Measure and draw a line across the back piece at 11¼ and 12 inches from the feet. This is the guideline for the seat. To mark where the base will go, measure and draw a line across the back piece at 1½ and 2¼ inches from the feet.

2 Place the mdf on a workmate or hard surface and clamp it firmly. Cut out all the pieces with a jigsaw. If you number or label each piece in pencil as you cut them out, the box seat will be easier to assemble later on.

3 Hold one of the side pieces against the edge of the back piece, aligning it at the top and bottom. Trace the thickness of the back piece by running a pencil along the back piece. Then, continue the seat and base guidelines onto the side piece. With a combination square, extend these two sets of lines across the side piece. Mark out the second side piece in the same way, placing it at the other end of the back piece.

4 Draw lines 1½ inches and 2¼ inches from the longest edge of the side piece. Mark pilot holes at regular intervals in pencil within the guidelines you have just drawn. (Remember, do not drill pilot holes too close to the edge of the mdf or it may split.) Then, using a No.5 drill bit, drill pilot holes at each point marked. Turn the side piece over and countersink each hole. Repeat on the second side piece.

PROFESSIONAL TIP

Before drilling, always break the surface of the wood or mdf with a bradawl. At the end of your drill bit is a point. By marking your pilot holes with a bradawl, you can rest the point at the tip of the drill bit in the small hole made by the bradawl. This means that you reduce the risk of your drill slipping on the surface. Remember, too, to hold your drill absolutely vertical at a 90° angle to the wood or mdf for a straight hole. When drilling, you should always maintain a firm grip and an even pressure on the drill.

CUTTING DIAGRAM

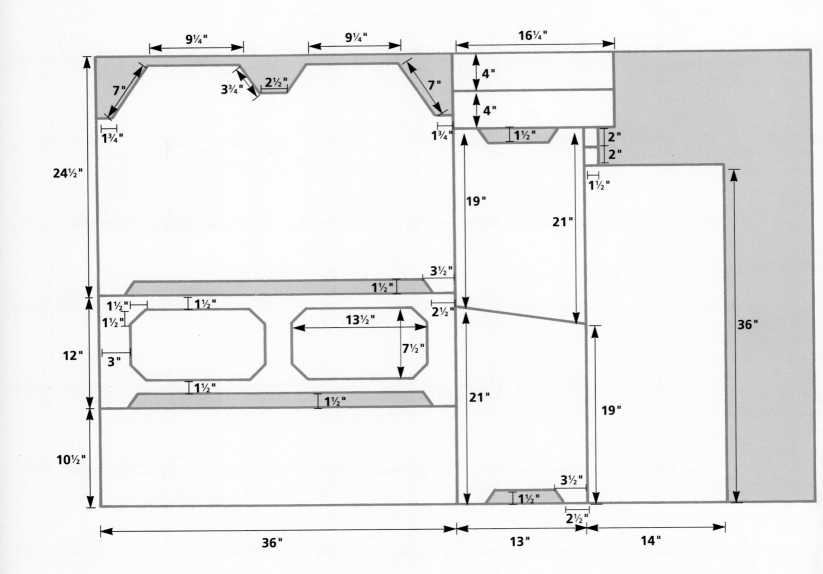

PUTTING IT TOGETHER - STEPS 5 TO 8

5 On one side piece, place a length of batten underneath the seat guide. Mark it so that it fits between the two vertical rows of guidelines and then cut the batten with a jigsaw. On each batten, measure 1 inch in from each end and drill a pilot hole at these points. Screw the batten in place with 1¼-inch screws. Do the same to the other side piece.

6 On the back piece, mark pilot holes at 5-inch intervals along the seat guidelines and the base guidelines. Drill these holes with a No.5 drill bit, then turn the back piece over and countersink each hole.

7 The back piece also needs a batten to support the seat. Measure and cut the batten so that if fits directly underneath the seat guidelines and is ¾ inch (the thickness of the mdf) in from each edge of the back piece. Drill pilot holes 2 inches in from each edge of the batten and one in the centre. Place the batten in position (underneath the seat guidelines and ¾ inch in from each edge) and attach it with three 1¼-inch No.6 screws.

8 The edges of the seat and the armrests are softened with a mitred corner. Lay the seat on your work surface with the eventual sitting side uppermost. Follow the instructions below to cut the front corners and repeat for each corner of the armrests.

MITRED CORNERS

To mitre any corner evenly, measure the same distance from the corner on the two edges. Join these lines and cut along the diagonal. The more you measure away from the corner, the larger the cut. In Step 8, we measure only 1 inch away from the two corners on the front of the seat (the long side closest to the pilot holes) and then cut along the diagonal line formed by joining the two points. Cutting away 1-inch corners softens the hard corners of the seat. To make it even more "child-friendly" sand the newly-cut edges.

PUTTING IT TOGETHER – STEPS 9 TO 12

9 On the front piece, you need to cut out the octagonal doors with a jigsaw. To get the jigsaw into the mdf, drill three holes close together, along the perimeter of the door where you will be adding hinges. Do this behind where a hinge will be fixed later. Drill the holes with the finest drill bit you have (the one used here is 2mm).

10 Then, using a bradawl or a very small screwdriver, carefully break through the wood between the holes. Ease the jigsaw blade into the hole you have made and cut out the door shape. Then repeat Steps 8, 9 and 10 for the other octagonal door.

11 Lay the front piece on your work surface and put the cut-out octagonal doors back in the holes. To add hinges to each door, place two hinges along the outside edge of the door and use a bradawl in the screw holes to break the surface of the wood. Attach the hinges with screws – the size of the screws will depend on the size of the hinges.

12 To assemble the box seat, hold one of the sides perpendicular to the back piece. Place a 1½-inch screw into each pilot hole and secure it in place. Repeat for the other side.

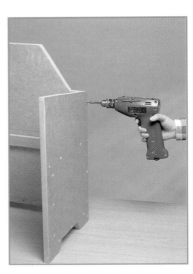

CUTTING DOORS

The doors are cut out of a single piece of wood, so they can be cut out in any shape or form. The combination of mdf and a jigsaw means that a rounded or curved door will be very easy to cut out. There are no limits to the shape of doors you can cut. A door in rounded petal shapes, for example, or two doors in a caterpillar curve will be easy to cut and you won't have any trouble making sure they fit. Make sure you thoroughly sand the cut edges of both of the doors and the front piece.

PUTTING IT TOGETHER – STEPS 13 TO 16

13 Lay the box seat on its back and place the base in position, aligning it with the guidelines on the back and side pieces. Attach the base by first screwing 1¾-inch screws into the pilot holes on the sides. Lift the box seat up and add screws through the pilot holes in the back piece.

14 To add the front piece, stand the box seat up and align the front piece so that its top edge is just under the seat guideline. Check this by adding the seat and checking it is level. If any of the legs are uneven, you can sand any of the legs back until the seat is level. Secure the front piece in postion with screws in the pilot holes on the sides.

15 To mark pilot holes to secure the seat, measure and mark pencil lines 3 inches and 3¾ inches from the front edge. Measure about 3 inches in from each short side and, between these marks, drill three evenly spaced holes inside the guidelines you have just drawn. Countersink these holes on the sitting side.

16 Rest the seat on the seat support and the front piece. Check that it aligns with the pilot holes and then secure it by inserting screws from the top of the seat into the front piece. Add further screws horizontally through the side pieces and through the back into the seat.

PROFESSIONAL TIP

A glued and screwed join is much stronger than one that is only screwed. But don't think that the more glue you use, the stronger the adhesion. Wood glue contains water and as it dries the water evaporates. If you have used too thick a layer of glue, gaps will appear at this stage. Use wood glue sparingly – apply an even, thin coating of glue to both surfaces to be joined. Then rub them together to create a suction between the two surfaces, which encourages the bonding.

FINISHING IT OFF – STEPS 17 TO 20

17 The armrests are 3 inches longer than the side pieces on which they rest. Mark them on the underside 1½ inches from each end and drill three holes centrally between these two marks. Align the marks with the ends of the side pieces so they are centrally placed. Countersink the holes and add screws to fix them to the side pieces.

18 Sand all the cut edges and cover all the screws with a quick-drying filler. Sand over the filler when it has dried and wipe over with a damp cloth to remove the dust. The seat is ready for painting: we used green for the seat, red for the armrests, blue on the doors and painted the rest in blackboard paint. Paint the seat with satin or matt varnish to protect the paintwork.

19 Cut out two pieces of mdf measuring 1½ by 2 inches for the door handles and sand away the sharp edges. Then paint them red and leave them to dry. To prepare the door for the handles, hold the handle against the door and mark the centre with a pencil mark. Drill a hole through the door at this point. Repeat for the other handle on the other door.

20 Apply wood glue to the back of the handle on the part that will cover the door. Hold the handle against the door and screw in a 1-inch long screw. Do the same for the other door.

WHICH PAINT?

When choosing the colours to paint your seat, take into account the colour of the room its going in, whether it's a bedroom, family room or play room. You could be a bit adventurous and try special paint that allows kids to draw in crayons over it, and then wipes clean (see your local paint supplier). Or try painting it with blackboard paint – one coat will usually give enough coverage. Don't forget a packet of coloured chalk and a duster, but if the chalk dust gets too much, you can wipe over it with a damp cloth.

VARIATION – MAKING A SEAT CUSHION

1 Measure the area of your seat. The one we made measured 13¾ by 35½ inches, but for accuracy you should measure your own. Mark out the measurements on a piece of cushion foam. Use the straight edges of the foam where possible and use a combination square to help keep the corners straight. To mitre the front corners, measure 2 inches from each corner and join the two lines up. Cut the foam with a sharp utility knife.

2 You need to cut your material to fit your foam seat. The size 33 by 41 inches represents twice the width of the foam seat plus 5 inches seam allowance and the length plus 5 inches.

3 Place the foam on your cut-out material. Pin together the short sides of the material and about 10 inches at each end of the long side. Remove the foam through the opening at the front and sew the seams. If you have more than ⅝ inch at the edges, trim the material or the seams will be too bulky. Measure across each mitred corner as in Step 1 (above) and sew these. Cut away the extra material at the corners.

4 At the front opening, sew a hem along each edge. Then turn the cushion cover inside out, so that the right side of the fabric is on the outside. Add your fastening to the front opening, in this case Velcro (see below). Replace the foam inside the cushion cover and press the Velcro together. Place the cushion on the box seat.

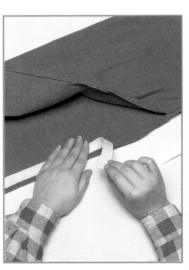

KEEPING YOUR CUSHION COVER CLOSED

You can make a cushion cover without making it removable, by sewing the opening by hand when you have put the cushion inside. However, when making anything for children, one of the most important things to consider is washability. And to get this cushion cover into a washing machine you have to be able to remove it. If Velcro doesn't appeal to you, there are other methods of keeping the cushion cover closed. These include a zipper, buttons and button holes, poppers, hooks and eyes, or tie fastenings.

CHILD'S VALET

Encourage children to be more tidy with this practical and novel valet. Complete with three shelves, two hanging rails, and a laundry bin, there's sure to be enough room for all kinds of toys and clothes.

EQUIPMENT

Pencil

Bradawl

Jigsaw

Combination square

Round plate to use as a guide

Tape measure or ruler

Clamp

Tenon saw

Power drill/ Screwdriver

No.5 drill bit and ¾-inch drill bit

2 sheets of cardboard, 24 x 38 inches

Spirit level

MATERIALS

To make a valet measuring 24 by 24 inches by 4 feet:

❖ Sheet of ½-inch mdf, 4 by 7½ feet

❖ Dowel, 4 feet long and ¾ inch in diameter

❖ Four castors, with screws

❖ Quick-drying filler and sandpaper

❖ Emulsion paint in bright colours and paintbrush

❖ Small round mirror (optional)

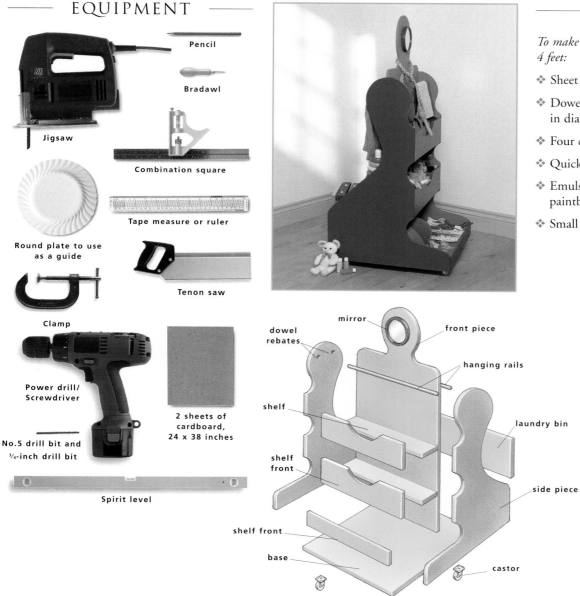

mirror

dowel rebates

front piece

hanging rails

shelf

laundry bin

shelf front

side piece

shelf front

base

castor

STARTING OUT – STEPS 1 TO 4

1 Copy the front piece template from page 92 onto a sheet of the mdf. To make the same size valet as the one made here, make each grid square 3 inches, so that the height from shoulder to floor is 38 inches and the valet's head shape is about 10 inches in diameter. Remember, you can use a plate or other round object as a guide to help you draw the head.

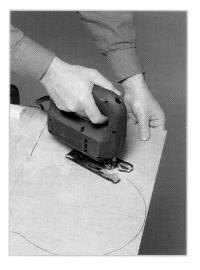

2 Copy the side piece template from page 93 onto a piece of cardboard, using the grid as a guide making each grid square 3 inches. Trace the cardboard template onto two pieces of mdf and cut out both pieces with a jigsaw.

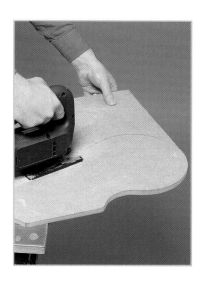

3 Mark and measure a square 24 by 24 inches for the base, using a combination square to keep your corners straight. Cut out the base with a jigsaw and draw a line ½ inch in from each edge. Mark and drill evenly spaced pilot holes within this guideline.

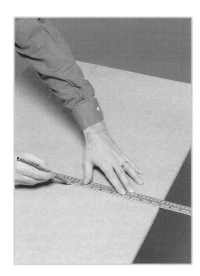

4 Measure, mark and cut out the four shelf fronts. Two measure 5½ by 23 inches, and the others are 2 by 23 inches and 8 by 23 inches. On the shelf fronts measuring 5½ by 23 inches, cut away curved handles. To do this, mark the centre and 3 inches in from one of the long sides. Place a round object (such as a plate) on this point as a guide and trace around it. Cut out the shape with a jigsaw and sand the edges.

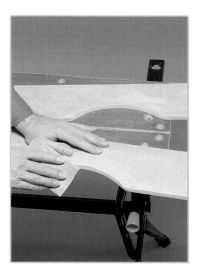

CUTTING CURVES

A power jigsaw is a particularly useful tool for cutting curves. Before cutting any wood or mdf with a jigsaw, make sure the piece is firmly clamped over the edge of a table or a workbench and check that the blade will not cut anything underneath. You need to look in front of the blade to judge the direction of the cutting line. You also need to maintain a firm and even pressure on the footplate to stop the blade vibrating. If you are finding it difficult to turn around a curve, press down on the jigsaw as you turn it.

PUTTING IT TOGETHER – STEPS 5 TO 8

5 There are two hanging rails on the valet, one on the front and one on the back. Mark on the dowel two lengths of 23½ inches each. Clamp the doweling to a work mate or hold it securely and cut out the lengths with a tenon saw. Lightly sand any rough edges of the wood.

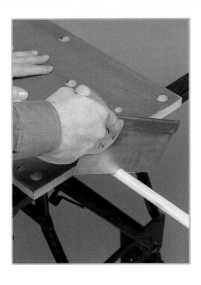

6 Measure and mark out the two shelves, which measure 4⅝ by 23 inches each. (The base of the lowest shelf and the laundry bin is formed by the square base piece.) Cut out the two shelves with a jigsaw.

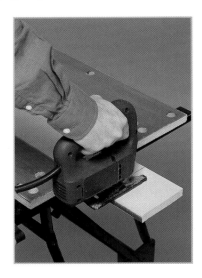

7 Place the template on top of one of the cut-out side pieces and copy the central guideline onto the mdf. This is where the front piece will be attached. Then copy each pair of guidelines that are perpendicular to the central guideline onto the mdf in the same way. On the other side piece, trace the lines on the reverse (see below).

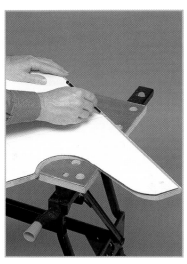

8 Using a bradawl, mark the position of the pilot holes on the mdf. They should be evenly spaced out, about 6–7 inches apart and 1 inch away from the top and the bottom on the central vertical guideline and about 2 to 4 inches apart on the horizontal guidelines. Alternatively, use the crosses on the template as a guide.

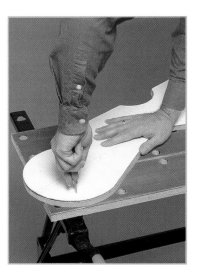

MARKING GUIDELINES

Marking guidelines on the two side pieces is an important step, as the front piece and the shelves are attached to them. Make sure that you draw the guidelines on one side piece and then turn the template over and copy them onto the opposite side of the other side piece. This is because when you stand the side pieces up, the guidelines need to face each other so that you can align the shelves and the front piece to them. It is important to check that the guidelines are accurate before you start drilling the pilot holes.

PUTTING IT TOGETHER – STEPS 9 TO 12

9 Mark the two points where the dowel will go on each of the side pieces, making sure they are exact on each side. One way to do this is to mark the wood through the cardboard template with a bradawl. Turn the template over and place it on the other side piece and place the bradawl through the same holes. Set the depth gauge to ¼ inch (see below) and use a ¾ inch drill bit to drill rebates for the doweling.

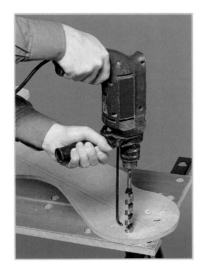

10 Using a No. 5 drill bit, drill all the pilot holes marked in Step 8 in both of the side pieces. When you come to assemble the valet, if you discover you have drilled too many pilot holes or drilled holes in the wrong places, you can disguise the mistakes with filler. These will be invisible once the valet is painted.

11 You can now start to assemble the valet. Due to its size, you may need to clear some floor space. Place a line of wood glue on the side of the front piece. Hold a side piece perpendicular to this and make sure the side edge of the front piece aligns with the central guidelines. Then put screws in each of the pilot holes within this guideline, checking that the front aligns with the side piece.

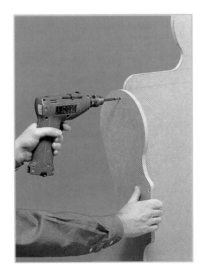

12 Place the doweling in the rebates on either side of the front piece. Hold the other side piece against the front piece and fit the doweling into the rebates. Then fix the side piece in place with a screw in each of the pilot holes.

PROFESSIONAL TIP

Power drills often come with an attachable depth gauge, which allows you to set the depth of the hole that you are drilling. If you do not have a depth gauge, wrap a piece of tape around the drill bit at the required depth. When you drill the hole, stop when the tape touches the wood or mdf. Drill bits have a sharp central point for precision location. Use a bradawl to make a hole first and position the bit's point in it. Then hold the drill absolutely vertical and proceed as usual to drill the hole.

FINISHING IT OFF – STEPS 13 TO 16

13 To attach the base of the valet, you may find it easier to turn the structure on its side. Before fixing a screw in each pilot hole, make sure the edge of the base is aligned with the side pieces.

14 Attach the two shelf bases by first holding them so that they align with the horizontal lines on the side pieces and with the pilot holes you made in Step 10. Screw in one side first, check that the shelves are straight with a spirit level, then screw in the other side. The shelf bases should not be flush with the sides of the valet, but about ½ inch in from the front.

15 Hold a shelf front so that the bottom edge aligns with the bottom of the shelf. Place a screw in the pilot holes on each side, and screw the shelf front in place. Secure the face of the shelf front to the bottom edge of the shelf by hammering in two evenly spaced panel pins. Do this for all the shelf fronts.

16 Sand all the rough edges of the valet with sandpaper, then wipe over with a damp cloth to remove the dust. Paint the valet with one or two coats of brightly-coloured emulsion paint. (If you wish, you can paint on a coat of matt varnish to protect the paintwork.) When the paint has dried, turn the valet on its side and attach the castors to the base with appropriate screws.

PROFESSIONAL TIP

If you decide not to paint your valet, don't worry about having pencil marks on the mdf. These all come off if you lightly sand the mdf. When cutting mdf with a jigsaw, the hot metal of the blade often "burns" the mdf, resulting in dark lines or marks on the cut edge. If any of these marks are visible on the assembled valet, they can be removed with sandpaper. In this project it is very important to sand all the corners as well as the rough edges to soften any sharp corners – and perhaps prevent a few bruises.

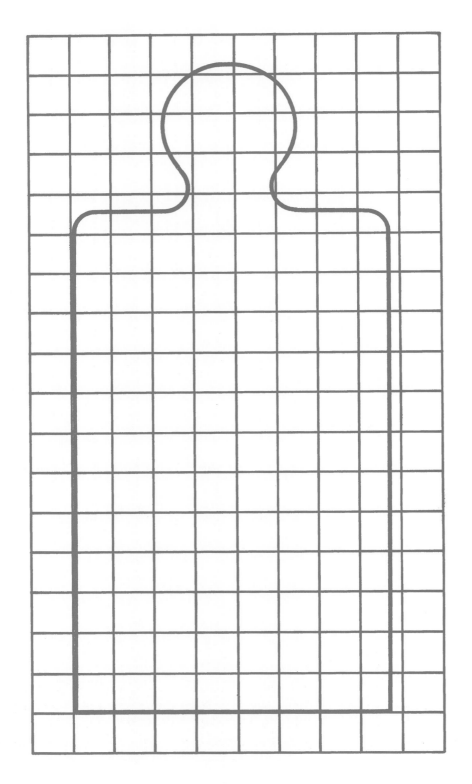

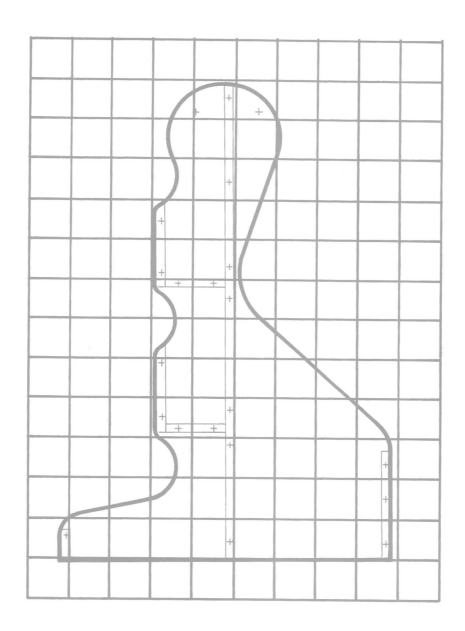

COPYING WITH A GRID

You can actually copy and enlarge any shape or picture with this method just by placing a grid over it. First, count the squares of your grid – the side piece for example is 8 squares wide and 12 squares long. To make the valet four feet high, we suggest you make each square 3 inches; but you can make the valet any size you want by changing the scale. Copy the enlarged grid onto a piece of cardboard. Then, working one square at a time, copy each line as it appears in each square of the grid onto your own grid.

BATHROOM ORGANISER

Bathroom bits and pieces have their own special compartments in this colourful fabric organiser. Suspended on the wall it makes an attractive bathroom accessory. Simply take it down, roll it up and pack it in your suitcase when you're going away.

EQUIPMENT

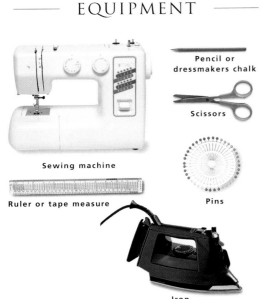

Sewing machine

Pencil or dressmakers chalk

Scissors

Pins

Ruler or tape measure

Iron

MATERIALS

❖ Piece of checked or any coloured fabric for the outside, 17½ by 25 inches

❖ Piece of fabric in a complementary colour for the inside, 15½ by 23 inches

❖ Piece of calico or any plain fabric for the pockets, about 23 by 26 inches

❖ Velcro, about 5 inches long, 1 inch wide

❖ Piece of plain fabric or ribbon for the loop and tie, 2½ by 25 inches

VARIATION

❖ Length of dowel or cane, 4½ feet long and about ⅜ inch in diameter

❖ Cutting mat and utility knife

❖ Leather thonging, about 16 inches long

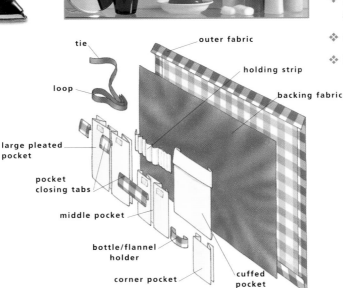

tie

loop

large pleated pocket

pocket closing tabs

middle pocket

bottle/flannel holder

corner pocket

outer fabric

holding strip

backing fabric

cuffed pocket

STARTING OUT – STEPS 1 TO 4

1 With a ruler and dressmaker's chalk or a pencil, measure and mark a rectangle 16½ by 24½ inches on the checked fabric and one 13 by 21 inches on the plain lining fabric. Cut these out with scissors.

2 To make the large pleated pocket, measure and cut out a rectangle of calico 9 by 16½ inches. Fold over a ¼-inch hem around the edges and press it with an iron. Then, machine-stitch the hem along one of the long sides.

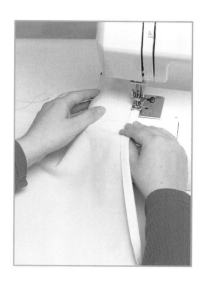

3 On an ironing board, fold the piece of calico in half and press it with an iron. Then fold it in half and in half again, so that the calico is divided into eighths, pressing each crease as you go. Spread the calico out so that you can see each eighth. To make the central pleat, pick up the first fold next to the central crease and place it on the central crease. Press with an iron. Do the same to the first fold on the other side of the central crease.

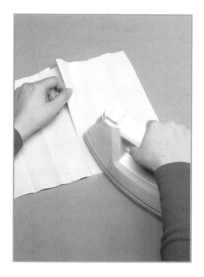

4 With the fabric still on the ironing board, make the outside pleats. To do this, pick up the second to last fold at one side and place it about ¼ inch in from the edge of the fabric. Then press it into place with an iron. Do the same to make the other outside pleat and press it with the iron. Then press the whole pocket to iron out all other folds.

ABOUT PLEATS

The purpose of pleating pockets is to make a pocket that remains folded flat when empty but has a deceptively large capacity when filled. In order to keep the shape of the pocket as neat as possible, make sure you iron the pocket flat before you pin it to the backing material. Also, pin the pleating closed at the top and bottom before you machine-stitch it to the material. The pleats are sewn flat along the bottom of the pocket, but will open out at the top when the pins have been removed.

PUTTING IT TOGETHER – STEPS 5 TO 8

5 Hold the pocket so that the hemmed side is on the top. To make the bottom of the pocket, fold the bottom 1 inch of the pocket under. Place the pocket on the plain backing fabric 1½ inches in from the side and bottom edge. Pin down the sides and the bottom of the pocket to the backing fabric.

6 Sew down the two sides on a sewing machine, removing the pins as you go. Then sew across the bottom, making two seams along the length for added strength.

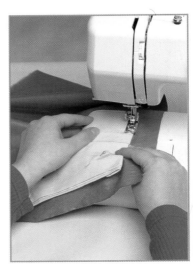

7 To make the pocket closing tabs, cut out two squares, 2¼ by 2¼ inches, from the checked fabric. Sew a ¼-inch hem along each side of the squares. Position the tabs above each side of the pocket, so that the top of each tab is ½ inch above the top of the pocket and the tab covers the pocket by about 1 inch. Pin the tabs to the backing material and then sew them in place.

8 To make the holding strip, measure and cut out a piece of calico 3½ by 9 inches. Turn over a ¼-inch hem and press it with an iron. Then sew a seam on each side of the strip. Position the strip so that the left side is 9½ inches from the left side of the backing material and the top of the strip is 2½ inches from the top. Sew the left-hand side of the holding strip on to the backing fabric.

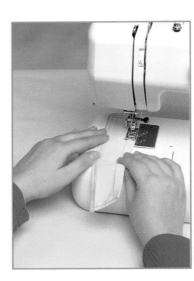

SEAMS

One way to add more decorative interest to this organiser is to use a contrasting thread for stitching some of the hems and seams, perhaps using a different colour for each pocket. If the fabric is likely to fray it can either be cut out with pinking shears, or sewn along the raw edge using a zigzag stitch and then folded over and sewn. You can also prevent fraying edges with a special liquid that bonds the fibres together (check your local supplier for availability), which is useful if a double fold would make the fabric too bulky.

PUTTING IT TOGETHER – STEPS 9 TO 12

9 Decide on the order of the items you will be keeping in the holding strip, as each segment is made to take individual items. Lay the first item next to the seam, and with it in place, sew a seam across the holding strip, next to it. Make sure that the item is gripped tightly by the material before you sew it. If it is too loose, the item will slip out. Add the next item and sew in the same way.

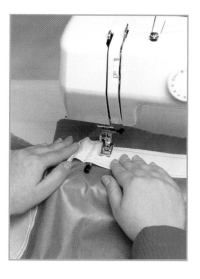

10 You do not have to limit yourself to small items – thicker items, such as lipsticks or small tubes of cream, can also be kept in the holding strip. Check that the strip is straight as you continue adding items and sewing them into place.

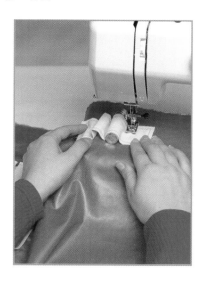

11 Next, make a bottle or flannel holder. To do this, measure and cut out a piece of checked fabric 2 by 7 inches. Turn over a ¼-inch hem on each side and press with an iron. Then sew a seam on each side on a sewing machine.

12 Place the left side of the bottle holder 6¾ inches away from the right-hand edge and about 3 inches from the bottom of the backing material and pin it in place. Then place the bottle or rolled flannel next to the seam and pin the right side of the holder in place. Sew the holder onto the backing, removing the pins as you go.

POCKETS AND LOOPS

If you find it awkward to sew the looped divisions with the pencils or brushes actually in place, then you can mark the stitching lines beforehand using a piece of tailor's chalk or a special dressmaker's "mark and erase" pencil and then sew them in place. Do not make these marks in pencil or in any type of marker that you cannot remove from the fabric. It is also a good idea to draw a base line onto the backing fabric to ensure that the loop or the pocket is attached in a straight line.

PUTTING IT TOGETHER – STEPS 13 TO 16

13 To make the pleated middle pocket, fold in half, and half again, creasing each fold as you make it. Then fold over a ¼-inch seam allowance and press with an iron.

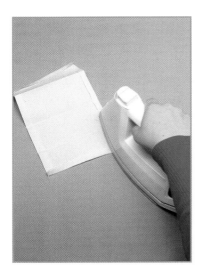

14 You should have a piece with three pressed creases. To make the central pleat, fold over two outer creases and place them onto the central crease. Press the pleat with an iron.

15 Position the middle pocket so that the top of the pocket is 2 inches underneath the holding strip. Fold the bottom of the pocket under ¼ inch and pin the pocket in place. Make sure the bottom of the pocket aligns with the bottom of the large pleated pocket.

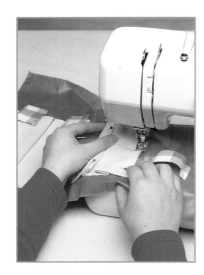

16 To make a pocket flap for the middle pocket, measure and cut out a piece of checked material 2 by 5 inches. Fold over a ¼-inch seam allowance and press with an iron before sewing the seams. Position the pocket flap directly over the pocket so that it overlaps the pocket by 1 inch. Pin and sew the flap into place.

PROFESSIONAL TIP

Don't be tempted to skip the ironing stage, especially on a project like this one, with many small pieces to be stitched. A flat, pressed fold will not usually unfold while you try to pin it. Also, seams will be less bulky to stitch under the needle once they have been pressed with a hot iron. For difficult fabrics, or when ironing pleats into a piece of fabric, use some starch to help you keep the creases. Take care to always check the type of material you use, as some fabrics are not suitable for ironing.

PUTTING IT TOGETHER – STEPS 17 TO 20

17 To make the cuffed pocket, measure and cut out a piece of calico 7 by 10 inches. To make the cuff, fold over ½ inch then 2 inches on one of the short sides and press with an iron. Then fold under a ½-inch hem on the remaining three sides and press with an iron.

18 Pin the cuffed pocket in position 1½ inches in from the right-hand edge and 1¾ inches down from the top of the backing strip. Machine-stitch into place.

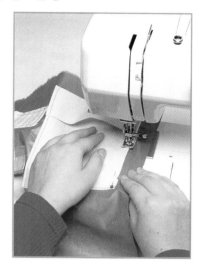

19 To make the corner pocket, cut a piece of calico 5 by 6 inches. On an ironing board, fold the material in half and in half again and then in half once more. Make sure you press each fold with an iron. Make two outer pleats only, following the directions in Step 4 and press these with an iron. Then, fold over ¼ inch at one long side and sew a decorative zigzag hem across it.

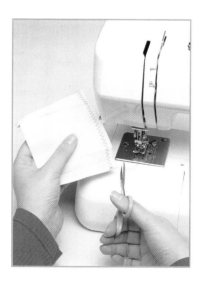

20 Position the corner pocket on the backing material so that the decorative hem is at the top and the pocket is positioned about 1 inch from the right-hand side of the material and from the bottom edge. Pin the pocket in place and then sew the pocket to the backing material.

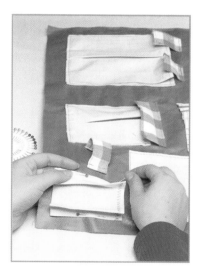

ZIGZAG OR STRAIGHT STITCH?

Straight stitch is suitable for most hems and seams and you can vary the length of the stitch to strengthen the stitching – the smaller the stitch, the stronger the seam. The zigzag stitch has many useful functions and is especially good for hemming, as it can prevent fraying. Zigzag also forms a decorative edging if a contrasting thread is used. A small zigzag stitch is a useful way of reinforcing a weight-bearing seam because the tension will be spread wider than on a straight row of stitching.

FINISHING IT OFF – STEPS 21 TO 24

21 Place the backing material with all the pockets on the checked fabric so that it is roughly in the middle. To sew each side, fold the checked material over ½ inch and another ½ inch, and pin down but do not sew yet. (Pin the short sides before the long sides if you intend to hang up the organiser, see page 102).

22 Make the loop and tie following the directions in the box below. Fold the smaller length in two and position both ends, as well as one end of the longer length, between the checked material and the plain fabric. Do this on the left side of the organiser and pin the layers of fabric together. The loop and tie should be facing toward the centre of the organiser.

23 Sew up the short sides of the organiser. When sewing the left side, make sure you fold the loop and the tie over, so they face away from the organiser, before you sew the seam. To keep the loop and tie in place, turn the organiser over, checked fabric uppermost. Fold the tie over fabric, so that it faces toward the centre, and sew a short seam across the loop and tie ¼ inch in from the edge.

24 Before you sew up the long sides, check the cane or dowel will fit if you are making the variation on page 102. Finally add strips of Velcro or poppers to the underside of each of the pocket flaps. Alternatively, you could secure each of the flaps with a button.

FASTENINGS

To make a loop and tie for the organiser, measure and cut out two pieces of plain fabric: one 2½ by 17 inches and the other 2½ by 7½ inches. Turn over ¼ inch on each long side of both pieces and press the seams with an iron. Then fold the two long sides over and press again. Finally, sew the seams together using zigzag stitch on a sewing machine. Alternatively, use the loop and a large decorative button, a long piece of Velcro, or simply tie it up with a ribbon or a long tie made out of the plain material.

VARIATION - HANGING IT UP

1 Hold the length of cane against the organiser allowing it to extend beyond the material by about 2 inches at each end. Mark the end point with pencil, hold the other length next to it and mark it the same length.

2 Cut the cane or dowel to the required length with a utility knife. You may not want to use split ends of cane, but for added interest, make sure that some of the knots in the cane are showing.

3 Insert a length of cane into the space between the edge of the fabric and the seam on the long side of the organiser. You may have to twist and turn the cane, as it should be a tight fit and the cane will have a few bumps in it. Do the same for the other long side with the other piece of cane.

4 Finally, measure and cut a piece of leather thonging about 32 inches in length. Tie each end to the cane at the top of the organiser, using a secure double knot. Hang the finished piece on the bathroom wall.

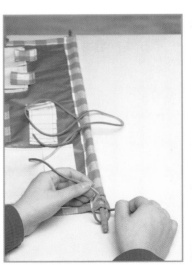

PROFESSIONAL TIP

By leaving the ends of the top and bottom seam open, you make a channel, allowing a piece of cane or dowel to be inserted. This allows the possibility of either hanging it up at home or being able to remove the rigid pieces of cane or dowel and roll it up neatly for travelling. The leather thong is just one way to keep your fabric organiser hanging up. You could also use a pretty matching ribbon, soft piping twine, or you could fix a pair of small wall hooks to the wall to hold the ends of the cane or dowel.

GLASS RACK

Keep wine glasses and tumblers safely and neatly arranged above your worksurface in this dual purpose rack. Simplicity itself to construct, it can be made to accommodate as many glasses as you like, making an attractive display that is ready to hand.

EQUIPMENT

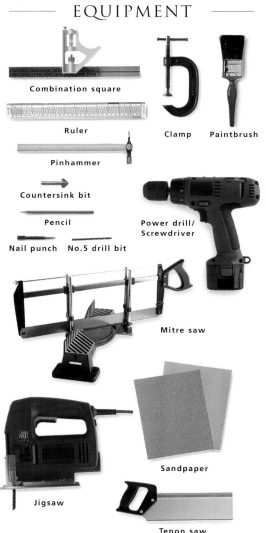

Combination square

Ruler

Pinhammer

Clamp

Paintbrush

Countersink bit

Pencil

Power drill/
Screwdriver

Nail punch   No.5 drill bit

Mitre saw

Jigsaw

Sandpaper

Tenon saw

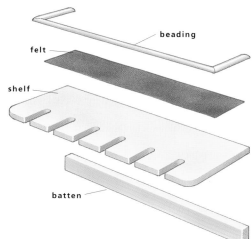

beading

felt

shelf

batten

MATERIALS

❖ Piece of ½-inch mdf, 8 by 27 inches (see note below)

❖ Batten, 1½-by-¾-inch, 27 inches long

❖ Piece of felt, 4 by 27 inches

❖ Beading, ¾ inch wide, about 3 feet long (see professional tip on page 107)

❖ Quick-drying wood-coloured filler

❖ Wood glue and spray adhesive

❖ Panel pins, ½ inch long

❖ Clear satin varnish

NOTE

If you have lots of glasses to store, why not consider making two shelves, to hang one above the other, or simply making one extra-long shelf.

STARTING OUT – STEPS 1 TO 4

1 If your mdf is not cut to size already, cut it now. Draw a line on the mdf, 3 inches in from one of the long sides. If the bases of your wine glasses are particularly wide, you may have to make this measurement larger (see below).

2 On the same long side, measure and mark the following points: $3\frac{3}{8}$, $4\frac{1}{4}$, $7\frac{3}{8}$, $8\frac{1}{4}$, $11\frac{3}{8}$, $12\frac{1}{4}$, $15\frac{3}{8}$, $16\frac{1}{4}$, $19\frac{3}{8}$, $20\frac{1}{4}$, $23\frac{3}{8}$, $24\frac{1}{4}$ inches. You should have six pairs of marks on the side of the mdf.

3 Rest the combination square on the edge of the mdf. With your pencil, draw a straight line from the first of the marks to the pencil line you drew in Step 1. Continue until you have drawn a line at each of the marks. Each pair of lines represents a wine glass holder.

4 Place the mdf on a work bench and clamp it in place, using a scrap of wood to protect it from being marked or damaged by the G-clamp. Carefully cut out each pair of lines with a jigsaw. Cut each line, then cut between them to form a long notch in the mdf.

PROFESSIONAL TIP

The glass rack is made to fit glasses you already have, so you must check that the notches are the right size for the stems of your glasses before you start cutting the mdf. A good way to tell if your glasses will fit is to measure the diameter of the stems of your glasses and then make sure the width of your notches is wider than the stems. Then draw the first notch and place the glass on the notch. Then check to make sure that the base of the glass does not overlap the position of the second notch.

PUTTING IT TOGETHER – STEPS 5 TO 8

5 Cut the length of batten to 27 inches with a tenon saw. Sawing is not always accurate, so even if your batten has already been cut to length at a timber yard, double check the length by holding it against the length of mdf and trim the batten to size.

6 Mark a point 2 inches in from each end of the batten, making sure it is in the middle of the width of wood. Drill a hole at each of these points, using a No.5 drill bit. On the same side, countersink each of these holes.

7 Lay the batten on its narrow side on top of the mdf shelf, so that it butts against the edge opposite the cut notches. Then, trace the width of the batten with a pencil. Measure and mark 2½ inches from each end, within the guideline you have just drawn. Then between these two points, mark two pilot holes, evenly spaced out, about 7 inches apart. Drill through the mdf with a No.5 drill bit and then countersink the two holes.

8 Place a wiggly line of wood glue along the narrow side of the batten and stick it to the mdf shelf. Make sure that you do not glue it to the side with the countersunk holes. Secure the batten to the shelf with a 1¼-inch screw in each pilot hole. Wipe away any excess glue.

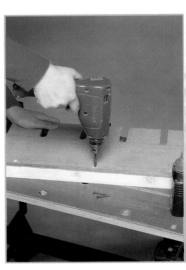

WOOD GLUE

Wood glue forms a strong bond between two pieces of wood, able to withstand great loads. However, it takes time for this strong bond to form, sometimes as long as 24 hours. If only glue was used to join wood together, you would have to wait a day before progressing to the next step. When joining wood together, a wiggly line of glue is used, so that the glue covers more of the surface of the wood. The join is then nailed or pinned to hold the wood together until the glue forms a bond, which is stronger than nails or pins.

PUTTING IT TOGETHER - STEPS 9 TO 12

9 Sand all the edges of the mdf and the batten. For a smooth finish, start with coarse sandpaper and then use fine. To sand the inside of the hanging glass notches, wrap a piece of sandpaper around a pencil. Cover screws with quick-drying filler and leave to dry.

10 To prevent the tumblers falling off the shelf, make a stop out of the beading. To measure the length you need, lay it across the shelf and make a pencil mark at the end of the beading. Using a mitre saw, cut the beading with both ends pointing inward.

11 To make a neat border, place the cut length of beading on the shelf about 4 inches from the back (see below). With the beading in place, measure the length of the two shorter ends. Make sure one end is mitred and the other is straight.

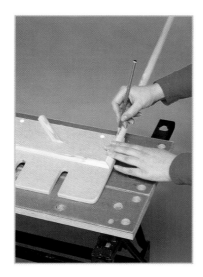

12 Hold the beading in position and measure the distance from the beading to the edge of the shelf, as well as the length. Cut this area out of the felt, adding an extra ¼ inch to the width measurement.

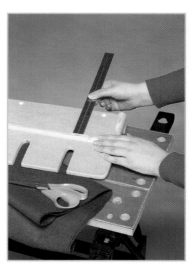

PROFESSIONAL TIP

Just as you had to check the size of the notches against the size of the stems and bases of the wine glasses, you also need to check the size of the border against the size of your tumblers. To do this, place the length of beading on the shelf and measure and cut its length as directed in Step 11. Then, hold the beading on the shelf at the recommended distance, 4 inches from the edge. Place the tumbler on its widest end within this border and check the fit. If it is too small, allow more than 4 inches.

FINISHING IT OFF ~ STEPS 13 TO 16

13 To help you place the felt accurately, trace around the beading while you hold it on the shelf. Then cover one side of the felt with spray adhesive and carefully place it between the guidelines you have drawn. Take care when doing this, as felt stretches easily. Fold the extra felt over the back of the shelf onto the batten.

14 Put a wiggly line of glue on the back of the beading and place the beading in position, using the guidelines to help you. Secure it with evenly spaced panel pins, about 4 inches apart.

15 Hide the heads of the panel pins by sinking them into the wood with a nail punch. Use wood-coloured filler to cover the panel pins and leave it to dry. If you use a quick-drying filler, it should only take about 10 minutes, but always follow the manufacturer's instructions.

16 Finally, paint the mdf and the strip of beading with clear satin varnish, taking care not to get any varnish on the felt. If you have a painted kitchen, you could paint the mdf and the beading in complementary or contrasting colours. If you do not use gloss paint, seal the painted surfaces with a coat of varnish.

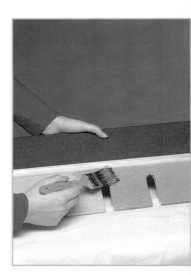

ALL ABOUT FELT

Felt provides a perfect surface for glassware – it indents slightly with the weight of the glass and prevents the glasses sliding around. It also provides a buffer to the hard surface of the shelf, which could cause the glasses to chip. Felt is a compressed material, unlike most other fabrics, which are woven. Because of this, felt is inclined to stretch, especially when dampened with glue. If stretching occurs when you smooth the felt on to the shelf, leave it to dry before trimming the edges to fit, in case the felt shrinks slightly.

CONVERSION TABLE

Inches to millimetres

	0	1	2	3	4	5	6	7	8	9	10	11	12	13	14	15	16	17	18	19	20	21	22	23	24	25	26	27	28	29	30	31	32	33	34	35	36	37	38	39	40
0	0	25	51	76	102	127	152	178	203	229	254	279	305	330	356	381	406	432	457	483	508	533	559	584	610	635	660	686	711	737	762	787	813	838	364	889	914	940	965	991	1016
1/8	3	29	54	79	105	130	156	181	206	232	257	283	308	333	359	384	410	435	460	486	511	537	562	587	613	638	664	689	714	740	765	791	816	841	867	892	918	943	968	994	1019
1/4	6	32	57	83	108	133	159	184	210	235	260	286	311	337	362	387	413	438	464	489	514	540	565	591	616	641	667	692	718	743	768	794	819	845	870	895	921	946	972	997	1022
3/8	10	35	60	86	111	137	162	187	213	238	264	289	314	340	365	391	416	441	467	492	518	543	568	594	619	645	670	695	721	746	772	797	822	848	873	899	924	949	975	1000	1026
1/2	13	38	64	89	114	140	165	190	216	241	267	292	318	343	368	394	419	444	470	495	521	546	572	597	622	648	673	698	724	749	775	800	826	851	876	902	927	952	978	1003	1029
5/8	16	41	67	92	117	143	168	194	219	244	270	295	321	346	371	397	422	448	473	498	524	549	575	600	625	651	676	702	727	752	778	803	829	854	879	905	930	956	981	1006	1032
3/4	19	44	70	95	121	146	171	197	222	248	273	298	324	349	375	400	425	451	476	502	527	552	578	603	629	664	679	705	730	756	781	806	832	857	883	908	933	959	984	1010	1035
7/8	22	48	73	98	124	149	175	200	225	251	276	302	327	352	378	403	429	454	479	505	530	556	581	606	632	657	683	708	733	759	784	810	835	860	886	911	937	962	987	1013	1038

The table above will help you convert any measurement in inches (imperial) to a measurement in millimetres (metric). For example, 11 inches is 279 mm, or 27.9 cm. To find out what 11⅜ inches is in millimetres, follow the column down to where it aligns with the left-hand column marked ⅜; so 11⅜ inches is 289 mm or 28.9 cm. The table also works in the opposite way. To find out what 60 cm is in inches, find 600 mm on the table. It is at the intersection of the 23 and the ⅝ column, which means that 60 cm is 23⅝ inches.

Drill bits are labelled by number or by size in millimetres or inches. The table below lists drill bit sizes used in this book and the metric and imperial equivalents.

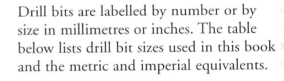

Drill bit size	Metric (mm)	Imperial (inches)
Number 1	5.80mm	⁷⁄₃₂ inch
Number 2	5.60mm	¹³⁄₆₄ inch
Number 3	5.40mm	¹³⁄₆₄ inch
Number 4	5.30mm	¹³⁄₆₄ inch
Number 5	5.22mm	¹³⁄₆₄ inch
Number 6	5.20mm	¹³⁄₆₄ inch
Number 7	5.10mm	³⁄₁₆ inch
Number 8	5.08mm	³⁄₁₆ inch
Number 9	5.00mm	³⁄₁₆ inch
Number 10	4.90mm	³⁄₁₆ inch

INDEX

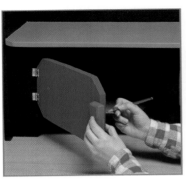

STORAGE: *Acknowledgements*

The author would like to thank and acknowledge the hard work of the following people:

Sally Walton for being my wife; **Stephanie Donaldson** for styling and allowing us into her home; **Paul Roberts** for his craftsmanship and **Steve Differ** for always being there with a helping hand.

Marshall Editions would also like to thank **Andrew Sydneham** for additional photography; **Philip Letsu** for design support; **Sophie Sandy** for the index; and **Sandro di Lucia** for his indispensable assistance.